French Verb Usage

A Direct Approach for American Students

French Verb Usage

A Direct Approach for American Students

WALTER STAAKS

Purdue University

SCOTT, FORESMAN AND COMPANY

Glenview, Illinois   London

TABLE OF CONTENTS

LE PASSÉ DÉFINI

ER

    parler   parl

                        ai   âmes
                        as   âtes
                        a   èrent

IR   finir   fin

                        is   îmes
                        is   îtes
                        it   irent

re   vendre   vend

                    (Endings same as for ___ IR verbs.)

Irregular Verbs and other verbs designated irregular in the
passé defini:

mourir   mour

                        us   ûmes
                        us   ûtes
                        ut   urent

être

fus fûmes
fus fûtes
fut furent

eus eûmes
eus eûtes
eut eurent

FOREWORD TO FOREIGN LANGUAGE TEACHERS

"To write, using the authentic patterns of the language *without conscious reference to English*" (italics mine), is one of the instructional objectives for modern foreign languages, as listed in the U. S. Office of Education's *NDEA Title III Guidelines*. I agree that this is an admirable aim. As a teacher of French I have, since long before the era of the "new key," conducted my classes in the foreign language to the extent that it was practical to do so, feeling that exposure to the target language without the interference of English would hasten the students' acquisition of ability to respond and think within the new linguistic framework.

Nevertheless I think it must be admitted by any teacher who has had his American students compose in French, orally or in writing, that it is a rare individual indeed who can escape entirely, in only two or three years of foreign language study, from the prison of his native tongue. However well he may have learned automatic responses, with variants, to particular linguistic situations, the necessity of expressing as yet unlearned patterns or relatively complex ideas sends him back to his own language and disastrous attempts to translate from it.

Sound overseas study programs have begun to change this, and the growth of FLES may also be expected to increase Americans' linguistic sophistication in the foreseeable future. But now and for some time to come, I believe we must recognize the restrictions which are imposed on our students' achievement in foreign languages by the relative brevity of their exposure to the second language and by what I would call the linguistic hardening of the brain which begins in most people in early youth.

French Verb Usage attacks this problem, insofar as verbs are concerned, by leading the student directly from whatever English verb form he has in mind to its equivalent in French. It can be assumed, I think, that the serious student, as he uses these shortcuts to the desired information, will gradually assimilate the French constructions and become progressively less dependent on the English-anchored bridge.

The aim of *French Verb Usage* is to provide at least one French equivalent (and often several) for any English verb group the student is likely to require. Explanatory notes accompany many of the examples.

I feel that the advantage of this manual over other books intended to acquaint students with French verb forms lies in the simplicity and the direction of its approach. A chapter on the verb **devoir** in a traditional grammar, to take an example, gives (often incompletely) the English translations of this perplexing verb in its various tenses; but how many students recall this information when they want to say in French, *"I should have stayed home"*? At best, they may remember what «**j'aurais dû rester**» means when they encounter it, but it is another matter for them to find the French when they need it. In such grammars, the explanations of **devoir** (and **falloir, pouvoir, vouloir,** etc.) may be systematic and thorough, the chapters on the subjunctive and the verb paradigms in the appendix may be orderly and logical, but I question their practical worth for the student who wishes to write something like, *"He might not have seen us."* In *French Verb Usage* he can find the combination quickly, under **MIGHT**.

A primary objective in teaching a foreign language is to rid students of the notion that the subject they are studying is a sort of code, whose one-to-one counterparts of English they are supposed to discover and memorize. I have tried to make this manual help serve this purpose by sprinkling nonliteral and idiomatic translations among the examples, not only where these have been required by the verb form itself, but in the "free" vocabulary which rounds out the illustrative sentences. In varying the latter, I hoped that the student using the book might derive secondary dividends in the form of increased vocabulary and a clearer realization that translation into a foreign language does not mean finding synonymous words, but rather choosing approximately equivalent ideas and expressions, whose components may bear little or no similarity to those of the original thought.

The plan of this book may be deplored by grammarians as unscientific, and it may be criticized by some teachers for its apparent complexity (why six sections instead of a single list, alphabetical by the first element of the group?). My answer to the first complaint would be that I am not concerned here with linguistic classifications, with differentiation between kinds of auxiliaries, with theoretical considerations of tense, aspect, mood, phase, etc., which are of interest to specialists but of little practical importance to students who simply want to learn to use a language rather than analyze it. To the second objection I would reply that a single list was seriously considered, and found to be unworkable. The divisions I finally chose, however arbitrary they may seem, are the result of much experimentation in an attempt to find the most efficient presentation of the material consistent with thoroughness of coverage, avoidance of excessive duplication, and confinement within reasonable bounds.

W. S.

TO THE STUDENT

French Verb Usage is addressed to you—the intermediate or advanced student who is faced with the problem of composing in French and is frustrated by an incomplete grasp of the French verb system.

The goal you are seeking is the ability to think and express yourself in the foreign language without having to translate from English. You will attain fluency in French only to the extent that you can formulate your thoughts in French, without reference to your native language.

But it is unrealistic to suppose that this facility can be acquired quickly. Two or three years of course work, during which French is but one of several subjects concurrently pursued, is not enough. Until further study, and/or the experience of living in a French environment, have brought you closer to control of French structure, the shortcuts offered by this manual will enable you to use even complicated verb forms confidently and correctly in your compositions. Furthermore, repeated use of these shortcuts will hasten both your mastery of the French verb and your freedom from the tedious and treacherous process of translation.

French Verb Usage is meant to be used like a dictionary. It consists of translations into French, in the context of complete sentences, of sample English verbs in all simple and compound forms and in all standard combinations with auxiliary, modal auxiliary, and semi-auxiliary verbs. In addition, it covers cases in which idiomatic French may use an auxiliary verb where none is present in English, or in which the choice of verb form in French is affected by accidental features (secondary verbs or other parts of speech) of the comparable English expression.

Although this manual contains some explanations of a grammatical nature, it is not a grammar, and does not take the place of one. Some familiarity with French verbs is assumed. This book shows you what form or combination of French verbs will translate a given English form, but it does not label each example with a tense name, and it does not present complete verb *conjugations*; these you are expected to know, or to look up elsewhere. You should be acquainted with the English names by which the parts and tenses of verbs are known, as this terminology is used in the explanations. You should also recognize the endings and possess some understanding of the French subjunctive; for, although many of the examples clearly show that a subjunctive is required, the book contains no systematic presentation of the rules governing that mode. You must be aware, for example, that a suggested translation of *"He did not come,"* alone, will not be valid for the context *"I am sorry he did not come,"* etc. It is obviously impossible to provide models of every imaginable combination of clauses.

The particular arrangement of this book makes it advisable to read the following instructions for use before attempting to use the manual.

INSTRUCTIONS FOR USE

I. The largest number of cases involve English combinations to which you will be guided by looking up, in the index, the first verb element of the group to be translated. These initial elements appear in the index in **CAPITALS**.

Examples:

For *"I would have had to wait"*	look up **WOULD**.
For *"Not having been warned"*	look up **HAVING**.
For *"You don't have to be an expert"*	look up **DON'T**.

II. The above procedure does not work when the critical element of the English combination is any of some two dozen verb forms which are preceded in the index by an asterisk.

Examples:

For *"Didn't you make him promise?"*	look up *make (not **DIDN'T**).
For *"We are going to fly"*	look up *going (not **ARE**).
For *"I was not supposed to work today"*	look up *supposed (not **WAS**).

A rapid inspection of the index will acquaint you with the verbs comprising this category.

III. Sometimes, particularly when one or more of these starred verbs are concerned, a complete model for a desired combination is not provided by any single example. (Separate listing of every imaginable union of auxiliary, modal, and semi-auxiliary verbs, even if possible, would entail an enormous amount of useless duplication.) It is then necessary to assemble information from different parts of the book.

Example:

"He might not have wanted you to get it fixed."

Look up successively **MIGHT**, *want, and *get. From these sources the translation can be composed:

«Il ne voulait peut-être pas que vous le fassiez réparer.»

This, of course, is an unusually complex example. It will seldom be necessary to consult as many as three different parts of the book in order to translate one English group.

IV. When the English verb form desired consists of only *one word* (*"when crossing the street,"* *"if I were you,"* *"taken aback by his reply, she. . ."* etc.), the word itself—since it might be any verb in the language—obviously cannot be included in the index. In these cases, locate the example through its grammatical designation: (English) *present participle, past subjunctive, past participle,* etc. These terms are *italicized* in the index.

If you are uncertain about these terms—only eight or nine of which are involved here—it will be helpful to glance through the subheads of Section I of the book, which contains all the one-word forms (except as noted in the introduction to the Section).

V. For negatives constructed with **DON'T, DOESN'T, DIDN'T,** and **WON'T,** see these words in the index (bearing in mind, however, paragraph II above). Other negative examples will be found among, or in a separate group immediately following, the corresponding affirmative forms.

VI. The remaining entries in the index are selected adjectives and adverbs whose translation, in association with verbs, may call for an auxiliary or a modal auxiliary verb, or may affect the choice of verb or tense, in French. For example: *"has* just *finished," "is not* necessary *to pay," "weren't* able *to learn."* A glance through Section VI, in which such examples are collected, will acquaint you with this resource.

WARNING! Before taking any verb form as a model, examine carefully all the sample sentences under its heading, to make sure you have selected the example which corresponds to the precise meaning you have in mind. This is especially important in the case of large groups like **HAD . . .ed, SHOULD, MUST,** etc.

The designation *". . .ed"* throughout this book is taken to represent any English past participle of whatever spelling; and *". . .ing"* stands for any English verbal form ending in those letters, regardless of its grammatical function.

In the examples, parentheses (   ) either enclose words which may optionally be added or show a nuance of meaning; brackets [   ] indicate alternate translations, and slashes / separate equally valid possibilities.

A Note on the Passive Voice

Although the manual includes many examples of translation of English passive forms, you may find it useful to digest the following general remarks on the use of the passive in French.

The passive is often more conveniently and more idiomatically rendered in French by using an active verb (with **on** as the subject when no other is indicated), or by a reflexive verb.

When the past passive is used in French, it is important to distinguish between past *event* and past *situation*. English does not always make this clear. *"She was invited"* might mean that she received the invitation then and there, at the moment we are talking about, and would then be translated «elle a été invitée [elle fut invitée; on l'a invitée]»; or it might mean that she was, by that time, an invited person, having received an invitation earlier. This idea would be expressed by «elle était invitée.» The past participle here has approximately the value of an adjective. Compare: *"the door was opened"* (= «la porte a été ouverte» [«on a ouvert la porte»]) and *"the door was open"* (= «la porte était ouverte»). The distinction is, of course, the basic one between the past indefinite and the imperfect, in the active voice as well as in the passive.

In French the personal indirect object of an active verb (such as **me** in «**il m'a raconté**») cannot, except in rare cases, become the subject of a passive verb. The French equivalent of *"I have been told"* is «**On m'a dit.**» **Je** cannot be used. «**Tout sera dit**» (= *"all, or everything, will be told"*), and «**l'histoire a été racontée**» (= *"the story was [has been] told"*) are grammatically and logically possible; but an *indirect personal object* is mandatory with verbs like **dire, donner, offrir, montrer, parler, raconter, accorder, défendre** *("forbid")*, **permettre, plaire, conseiller**, etc. (We except, naturally, the extraordinary situations in which a person is, actually, transferred to another person's control, offered as a slave, displayed in an exhibit, or otherwise treated as a piece of merchandise.)

Thus, a word-for-word translation is IMPOSSIBLE for such English forms as: *"He will be given the money," "I was advised to leave," "She has been permitted to disembark,"* etc. Use **on**, not the passive voice, in expressing ideas of this kind.

A Note on the Agreement of Past Participles

Stated as concisely as possible, the rules governing the agreement of the past participle of a verb in a compound tense are the following:

1. If the auxiliary verb is **avoir**, the past participle agrees in gender and number with a *preceding direct object*, and not with any other noun or pronoun.

2. If the verb is conjugated with **être** and is not reflexive (or reciprocal), the past participle agrees with the subject, wherever it may be. This of course applies to any verb in the passive voice.

3. If the verb is used reflexively or reciprocally, its compound tenses are formed with the auxiliary **être**, but the rule of agreement is the same as that for verbs conjugated with **avoir**.

Examples:

No Agreement

1. **Elle a raté ses examens.**
   Il leur a raconté une fable.

2.

3. **Ils se sont parlé.**
   Elle s'est offert une montre.
   Nous nous sommes rendu compte.

Agreement

1. **Voici les modèles qu'elle a choisis.**
   La tondeuse? Ils nous l'ont rapportée hier.

2. **Elle est revenue.**
   Que sont devenus les enfants?
   Ils ont été expulsés.

3. **Elle s'est levée.**
   Ils se sont regardés.
   Ils s'étaient enfuis.
   La voiture qu'il s'est achetée.

Past participles used adjectivally agree with the noun or pronoun to which they refer: «**Encouragés par cette réussite inattendue, ils poursuivaient l'attaque.**»

This summary does not cover every foreseeable question of agreement. There are exceptional cases and fine points, elucidated in any thorough grammar. Some of these secondary rules are noted, or inferable from the illustrative sentences, in this manual. The principles stated above are, however, dependable guides in the great majority of problems of participial concordance.

A Note on Interrogatives

In popular spoken French, interrogation seems to be more commonly indicated by intonation than by word order. This is true not only in such acceptable patterns as «**Elle est de retour?**» (which has an exact counterpart in English *"She's back?"*), but even in incorrect constructions like «**Où elle était?**» (for *"Where was she?"*)— undoubtedly a further shortening of the already elliptical «**Où qu'elle était?**» Despite the existence of these ungrammatical forms at certain levels of communication I do not recommend them for imitation.

French Verb Usage

A Direct Approach for American Students

Section 1
ENGLISH ONE-WORD FORMS

The eight subdivisions of this section cover the verb forms which consist of only one word in English, not counting *to* or *not*. These include: (English) present indicative, preterit (past), imperative, present subjunctive, past subjunctive, present infinitive, present participle and gerund, and past participle.

Exception: If the single word is an auxiliary or modal auxiliary which implies or replaces an antecedent verb (e.g., *Yes, we have, No, she doesn't, They might,* etc.), it is located with the other examples of that auxiliary.

A. English Present

1.	We live on the top floor.	**Nous habitons le dernier étage.**
2.	Most children hate spinach.	**La plupart des enfants détestent les épinards.**
3.	His American accent grates on my nerves.	**Son accent américain me tape sur les nerfs.**
4.	The firm hires only bilinguals.	**La maison n'engage que des personnes bilingues.**
5.	If you find what you want. . .	**Si vous trouvez ce que vous désirez. . .**
6.	What if you lose?	**Et si vous perdez?**
7.	When he plays cards he forgets what time it is.	**Quand il joue aux cartes il oublie l'heure.**
8.	I would like to be there when he opens that package.	**Je voudrais être là quand il ouvrira ce paquet.**
9.	I'll remember it as long as I live.	**J'en garderai le souvenir tant que je vivrai.**

English present is translated by French future after such conjunctions as **quand, lorsque, dès que, tant que,** and **aussitôt que** (but not **si**) when future time is implied (8 and 9).

10.	A prize will be awarded to the one who submits the best plan.	**Il sera attribué un prix à celui qui proposera le meilleur plan.**

Futurity of an event or situation is also reflected by the French choice of tense in relative clauses such as the above.

11.	I think it is time to go back.	**Je crois qu'il serait [est] temps de rentrer.**
12.	I have a request to make of you.	**J'aurais une demande à vous faire.**
13.	How I need advice!	**Que j'aurais besoin de conseils!**

The conditional may be used to soften an assertion. With **11**, **12**, and **13**, compare English *might be, . . .if I may, could use.*

14.	By his account, he is the best artist in the country.	**D'après lui, il serait le meilleur artiste du pays.**
15.	You are his father? Incredible!	**Vous seriez son père? Pas possible!**

The conditional may translate English present to convey skepticism or incredulity.

16.	If you hurry you can catch up with them.	**En vous dépêchant vous pourrez les rattraper.**

The **en** + present participle construction is a possibility to keep in mind when *if. . .* has approximately the meaning of *by . . .ing,* and if both clauses have the same subject. See also **17**.

17.	He whistles while he works.	**Il sifflote en travaillant.**
18.	If he loses his balance he's done for.	**Qu'il perde l'équilibre, et c'en est fait de lui.**

In this subjunctive variant of the normal **si** + present indicative, the literal meaning of the French is, of course, *Let him (so much as) lose. . . .*

B. English Preterit (Simple Past)

(For convenience, this division also includes some English past subjunctives [**38, 49, 50**] since these, except in the case of the verb *be* [see **76-80**], are identical in spelling with the preterit forms.)

19.	She tripped over the curb.	**Elle a trébuché sur la bordure du trottoir.**
20.	His motorcycle struck a bridge abutment.	**Sa moto a percuté [percuta] une culée de pont.**
21.	The French team scored first.	**L'équipe française marqua les premiers points.**
22.	I asked him what he did for a living.	**Je lui ai demandé comment il gagnait sa vie.**

23.	On Sundays we played tennis.	**Le dimanche nous jouions au tennis.**
24.	It was a brand new dress.	**C'était une robe toute neuve.**
25.	There were flowers everywhere.	**Il y avait des fleurs partout.**
26.	They were never happy in Rome.	**Ils n'ont jamais été contents à Rome.**
27.	Last week's game was much more exciting.	**Le match d'il y a huit jours a été beaucoup plus passionnant.**
28.	He was tired.	**Il était fatigué.**
29.	He was suddenly very gay.	**Il fut tout à coup très gai.**
30.	She had a lot of friends.	**Elle avait beaucoup d'amis.**
31.	I had some bad news this morning.	**J'ai eu une mauvaise nouvelle ce matin.**
32.	Seeing what he had done, he was ashamed.	**Voyant ce qu'il avait fait, il a eu [eut] honte.**
33.	She didn't tell me what she wanted.	**Elle ne m'a pas dit ce qu'elle voulait.**
34.	I knew you hadn't forgotten.	**Je savais bien [j'étais sûr] que vous n'aviez pas oublié.**
35.	He found out that I had left.	**Il a su que j'étais parti.**

English simple past is regularly rendered by the past indefinite (**passé composé**) in spoken or informal modern French, although the third person past definite (**passé simple**) is normal in narration and, far from being limited to literary style, is commonly found in newspaper articles.

Notice, however, that either context (second clause of **22**) or intended meaning may call for the imperfect, the tense which normally refers to a situation existing at a past moment, or to a habitually repeated action, rather than to a particular occurrence.

Many verbs, by the nature of their meaning, usually imply unspecified duration, conditions, attitudes, and the like; and therefore, these verbs are found more often in the imperfect than in the past indefinite. This group of verbs includes the French equivalents of:

admire	doubt	have	long for	seem
be	expect	hope	long to	suspect
believe	fear	know	love	think
contain	feel	imagine	prefer	understand
desire	hate	like	regret	want
				wonder

But the verbs of this type are not to be put automatically into the imperfect. The fundamental difference between imperfect and past indefinite (or past definite) must be respected. Thus French uses the past indefinite (or past definite) of these verbs when the intention is to indicate that the condition, attitude, or state of mind *began* at the past moment in question—that a *change* took place. Compare **28** and **29**. The first describes a past state; the second notes a change (*was = became*). Similarly, **30** tells of a circumstance, while **31** announces an event (*had = received*). Note also **35**: «il a su» means *he came into possession of information*—not merely *he knew.*

36. She said she would believe it when she saw it.

Elle a dit qu'elle le croirait quand elle le verrait.

Compare this sentence with **8** and **9**. Just as English present is translated by French future in certain clauses referring to future time, English past is rendered by French conditional, in parallel constructions, to indicate the futurity of the dependent verb with respect to the (past) time of the main verb.

37. It was you who caught the mistake.

C'est vous qui avez relevé l'erreur.

The past time of the action is shown in the relative clause, while the present tense of the main verb in French logically indicates the continuing applicability of the identification. Compare with the English *You are the one who.* . . .

38. If he ate less, he would feel better.

   a. **S'il mangeait moins, il se sentirait mieux.**

   b. **Il mangerait moins, il se sentirait mieux.**

39. If he ate it, he doesn't remember doing so.

S'il l'a mangé, il ne s'en souvient pas.

40. We don't know if he ate it or not.

Nous ne savons pas s'il l'a mangé ou non.

Compare examples **38, 39,** and **40**. In **38**, the verb of the result clause is in the present conditional, in both languages; the imperfect is then the standard tense for the *if* clause in French (but note the possible alternative, without **si**). English also permits here *if he were to eat less* (see **393**). In **39**, English *if he ate* means *if it is true that he ate* or *if indeed he ate [did eat]*. In **40**, *if* could be replaced by *whether*. The last two cases require the past indefinite in French.

41. You should have written to him as I advised you to do.

Vous auriez dû lui écrire comme je vous l'avais conseillé.

42. I told you he would refuse.

Je vous avais bien dit qu'il refuserait.

French is often more logical and precise than English in the choice of tense. In **41** (*advised*) and **42** (*told*), a "past past" is really meant. In **41** the decision not to write, itself past, was preceded by advice to the contrary, and French marks this chronology by using the pluperfect. In **42** the French sequence of tenses makes it clear that the refusal has already taken place, following a prediction to that effect. **Je vous ai dit. . .** would simply be a reminder of what the speaker has stated before, with the occasion for refusal presumably still in the future.

43. When he arrived home, he found his sister waiting for him.

Arrivé chez lui, il y trouva sa sœur qui l'attendait.

The combination *when* + preterit, provided the main clause has the same subject, is often reduced in French to the past participle alone, if the verb in question is one of the **être** verbs marking change of place.

44.	An incident which occurred Saturday evening. . .	**Un incident survenu samedi soir. . .**

Similarly, the past participle alone frequently fills the role of English subject + preterit verb in relative clauses. (Compare **189-191**.) This sort of ellipsis is not confined to **être** verbs: **Un article paru au** Journal officiel. . . = *An article which appeared in the* Journal officiel. . . .

45.	According to him, the Russians invented everything.	**A l'en croire [D'après lui], les Russes auraient tout inventé.**

Here the conditional perfect, like the present conditional of **14**, conveys the speaker's disavowal of the assertion.

46.	Four months later, he married her.	**Quatre mois plus tard, il l'épousait.**
47.	At precisely six o'clock, the alarm went off.	**A six heures précises la sonnerie se déclenchait.**

The special use of the imperfect in **46** and **47**, variously called the narrative, or dramatic, or pictorial imperfect, seems to violate the general rule that *events* are told in the past indefinite or past definite, while the imperfect is reserved for *situations* in the past. Usually preceded by some kind of indication of time, this exceptional but by no means rare imperfect is used either to emphasize the date or moment of the occurrence in question, or to make the action or event more vivid.

48.	He hummed as he walked along.	**Il chantonnait en se baladant.**

The **en** + present participle construction is one to keep in mind when *as*. . . has approximately the meaning of *while. . .ing,* and if both English clauses have the same subject. Compare **17**.

49.	It's time someone told him off.	**Il est temps que quelqu'un lui dise son fait.**
50.	An officer who behaved like that would be broken.	**Un officier qui se comporterait de la sorte serait cassé.**

The French conditional is used (here translating an English subjunctive) because the behavior in question is hypothetical, not factual. Compare *If an officer behaved [were to behave]*. . ., and note the two translations offered for **38**.

51.	(Whereupon) everyone applauded.	**Et tout le monde d'applaudir.**

Example **51** illustrates the "narrative infinitive," usable when the action described is closely linked consequentially to what has just preceded. The words **et** and **de** are indispensable parts of the construction.

C. English Imperative

52.	Move forward!	**Avancez!**
53.	Hurry (up)!	**Dépêchez-vous! [Dépêche-toi!]**
54.	Lend it to them.	**Prêtez-le-leur.**
55.	Be reasonable.	**Soyez raisonnable.**
56.	Please [Be so kind as to] hand me that brush.	**Veuillez me passer cette brosse.**
57.	Help yourself.	**Servez-vous.**
58.	Write in French:	**Ecrivez [Ecrire] en français:**
59.	Bring to a boil.	**Porter à ébullition.**
60.	Apply to the caretaker.	**S'adresser au concierge.**
61.	Take it or leave it.	**C'est à prendre ou à laisser.**
62.	Take this to Mr. Chapelain.	**Vous porterez ceci à monsieur Chapelain.**
63.	Somebody get this stuff out of here!	**Qu'on me débarrasse de tout cela!**
64.	Nobody leave this room!	**Que personne ne sorte!**

English one-word second person imperatives have an exact counterpart in French. There is no subject pronoun, except in case of special emphasis (the **vous** in **53** is the reflexive object pronoun). Note, however (**58, 59,** and **60**) that general orders or directions are frequently expressed by the infinitive. Instructions to a particular individual or group may occasionally be given in the future tense (**62**); compare with the English *You will do as I say*.

The one-word third person command or wish exemplified in **63** and **64** is relatively rare, and is linked almost exclusively to such indefinite pronouns as *someone, nobody, everybody*. This type of command might also be considered a subjunctive in English (see **65** and **66**), and its French equivalent is in the subjunctive. See also **HAVE something . . .ed (431** and **432)** and **LET (681** and **682).**

D. English Present Subjunctive

65.	Someone look after the baggage.	**Que quelqu'un s'occupe des bagages.**
66.	Everyone be quiet!	**Que tout le monde se taise!**

See also **63** and **64**.

67.	Heaven help us!	**Puisse le ciel nous aider!**
68.	God forbid!	**A Dieu ne plaise!**
69.	Long live coffee breaks!	**Vive la pause café!**
70.	So be it.	**Soit. [Ainsi soit-il.]**

71. Come hell or high water.	a. **Advienne que pourra.**
	b. **Quoi qu'il advienne.**
72. Be they ever so poor. . .	**Si pauvres qu'ils soient. . . [Si pauvres soient-ils / Tout pauvres qu'ils soient / Pour pauvres qu'ils soient]**
73. I shall say nothing about it lest he misunderstand my motives.	**Je n'en parlerai point de peur qu'il ne se méprenne sur mes motifs.**
74. It is essential that he go to London for a few days.	**Il est de toute nécessité qu'il aille passer quelques jours à Londres.**
75. I recommended that he buy traveler's checks.	**Je lui ai conseillé d'acheter des chèques de voyage.**

The one-word English present subjunctive can usually be translated by the French subjunctive, although an infinitive construction may be more natural in some cases (75).

E. English Past Subjunctive

76. If I knew his address, I would send him a card.	Si je savais son adresse, je lui enverrais une carte.
77. If he were here, he could help us.	S'il était ici, il pourrait nous aider.
78. Even if he were here, he couldn't help us (out of this situation).	a. Même s'il était ici, il ne pourrait pas nous dépanner.
	b. Quand même il serait ici; il ne pourrait pas nous dépanner.
	c. Il serait ici, qu'il ne pourrait rien faire pour nous.
79. Were he the richest man on earth, I wouldn't marry him.	Il serait [Fût-il] l'homme le plus riche au monde, je refuserais toujours de l'épouser.
80. Were it not for social security, he would have trouble making ends meet.	N'était [Sans] la sécurité sociale, il aurait du mal à joindre les deux bouts.

The most common use of English past subjunctive is designation of a condition contrary to fact. *Be* is the only English verb whose past subjunctive form differs from its preterit. The most frequent French equivalent is the imperfect indicative in a **si** clause; possible variants are suggested in **78b, 78c, 79,** and **80.** Note the omission of **si** when the conditional is used. See also **1132.**

F. English Present Infinitive

81. To understand is to forgive.	Comprendre, c'est pardonner.
82. Nothing to report.	Rien à signaler.
83. To avoid disappointment, reserve your seat today.	Pour éviter une déconvenue, réservez votre place dès aujourd'hui.

84.	It is hard to adjust [get used] to Saturday classes.	Il est difficile de [C'est dur de] s'habituer aux cours de samedi.
85.	Her handwriting is hard to read.	Son écriture est difficile à lire.
86.	Invite him to go with us.	Invitez-le à nous accompagner.
87.	You were right not to protest.	Vous avez bien fait [Vous avez eu raison] de ne pas protester.
88.	He is too lazy to put up the storm windows.	Il est trop paresseux pour monter les contre-fenêtres.
89.	I have quite a lot to do.	J'ai pas mal de choses à faire.
90.	I prefer not to go out today.	Je préfère ne pas sortir aujourd'hui.
91.	The problem is (how) to get them back.	Le difficile, c'est de les récupérer.
92.	All our attempts to locate the document ended in failure.	Toutes nos recherches en vue de retrouver le document ont été infructueuses.

A full treatment of the syntax of the infinitive occurring independently of auxiliary verbs is outside the scope of this book. As is apparent from **81-92**, in which English *to* forms are translated by French infinitives, the problem is often not one of finding the corresponding verb form, but of determining what preposition, if any, should precede it. On this subject, a grammar should be consulted.[1]

Common combinations of English infinitives with auxiliary or modal auxiliary verbs, as well as numerous examples of infinitives following semiauxiliaries, are found in other sections of this manual.

93.	Show me what to do.	Montrez-moi ce qu'il faut faire.
94.	Tell me where to meet you.	Dites-moi où je dois vous retrouver.
95.	Wire him to come at once.	Télégraphiez-lui qu'il vienne tout de suite.
96.	The lake is too cold to swim in.	Le lac est trop froid pour qu'on s'y baigne.
97.	What a stupid thing to say [to do]!	Non, mais quelle bêtise!

Sentences **93-97** contain examples of English infinitives which are better translated [or translatable only] by changing the construction.

98.	Why walk when we have a car?	Pourquoi aller à pied, puisque nous avons la voiture?
99.	Why not stay home?	Pourquoi ne pas rester [ne resterions-nous pas] à la maison?
100.	He does nothing but read [All he does is read] science fiction.	Il ne fait que lire [Il n'a pas d'autre occupation que de lire] de la science fiction [science romancée].

[1]An excellent exposition of the translation of prepositions into French is Clifford H. Bissell's *Prepositions in French and English* [Richard R. Smith, New York, 1947].

101. Me do the cooking? Are you out of your mind?	**Faire la cuisine, moi? [Que je fasse la cuisine, moi?] T'es cinglé peut-être?**

The English verb forms in **98-101**, lacking the marker *to*, are not called infinitives by all modern grammarians and linguists, but it is convenient for the purposes of this book to give them this traditional classification.

G. English Present Participle and Gerund

102. Being rich, he had many friends.	**Etant riche, il avait beaucoup d'amis.**
103. He went away, suspecting nothing.	**Il s'en alla ne se doutant de rien.**
104. He showed us a stairway leading to the attic.	**Il nous a indiqué un escalier conduisant au grenier.**
105. On seeing me, he rose and held out his hand.	**En me voyant, il se leva et tendit la main.**
106. I made him happy by accepting his offer.	**Je lui ai fait plaisir en acceptant sa proposition.**
107. Let's play a game of chess while waiting.	**Faisons une partie d'échecs en attendant.**
108. Be polite when speaking to visitors.	**Soyez poli en parlant aux visiteurs.**

English . . .*ing* has a counterpart in the French . . .**ant** in such constructions as the above. (Note the several values of **en** shown in **105-108**.) But the French present participle is much less versatile. Read on.

109. Think before acting.	**Réfléchissez avant d'agir.**
110. She is afraid of gaining weight.	**Elle craint [a peur] d'engraisser.**
111. He went on his way without turning around.	**Il continua son chemin sans se retourner.**
112. After examining the statuette, he set it on the table.	**Après avoir examiné la statuette, il la posa sur la table.**

Though . . .*ing* preceded by a preposition translatable by **en** can normally be rendered by the . . .**ant** form, all other French prepositions require the infinitive (**109-111**), and **après** requires the perfect infinitive (**112**).

113. He spent the evening painting.	**Il a passé la soirée à peindre.**
114. I had trouble understanding him.	**J'ai eu du mal à le comprendre.**
115. That's saying a great deal.	**C'est beaucoup dire.**
116. There is no denying it.	**Il n'y a pas à dire.**
117. Reading the assignment is not enough; you must study it.	**Il ne suffit pas de lire la leçon; il faut l'étudier.**
118. Oddly enough, she enjoys cleaning house.	**Chose curieuse, elle trouve du plaisir à faire le ménage.**

Examples **113-118** are typical constructions in which . . .*ing*, not following a preposition, must be rendered by an infinitive in French.

119.	He spoke in a trembling voice.	**Il parlait d'une voix tremblante.**
120.	The girl, trembling with fear, placed her hand on the doorknob.	**Tremblant de peur, la jeune fille posa la main sur la poignée de la porte.**

Differentiate between the adjectival use of an . . .*ing* word (**119**), where the French counterpart agrees with the noun in gender and number, and the participial . . .*ing* (**120**), whose French equivalent is invariable.

121.	There she is, sitting in the last row.	**La voilà, assise au dernier rang.**
122.	A Siamese cat lying by the fireplace glared at me.	**Un chat siamois couché devant la cheminée me fixa d'un regard hostile.**
123.	Leaning on the railing, she was watching the seagulls circling behind the ship.	**Accoudée au garde-fou, elle regardait les mouettes qui suivaient le bateau en tournoyant.**

A number of . . .*ing* forms describing position or situation are translated by the adjectival past participle. The verbs in this category include:

accoudé *(leaning [on elbow])*	**couché** *(lying)*
accroché *(hanging)*	**cramponné** *(clinging)*
accroupi *(crouching, squatting)*	**domicilié** *(residing)*
addossé *(leaning [with the back])*	**étendu** *(lying)*
agenouillé *(kneeling)*	**penché** *(leaning, bending)*
appuyé *(leaning)*	**pendu, suspendu** *(hanging)*
assis *(sitting)*	**perché** *(perching)*
caché *(hiding)*	**vautré** *(sprawling)*

See also **339** and **386**.

124.	I can understand his not wanting that responsibility.	**Je comprends [conçois] bien qu'il ne veuille pas de cette responsabilité.**
125.	There is little likelihood of her changing her mind.	**Il est peu probable qu'elle change d'avis.**
126.	It's like actually being at the theater.	**C'est comme si on était vraiment au théâtre.**
127.	Those coming by car should take route 152 out of Orléans.	**Ceux qui viennent en voiture doivent emprunter la 152 à partir d'Orléans.**
128.	He took the first bus leaving for Miami.	**Il prit le premier car en partance pour Miami.**
129.	That being the case, I'd as soon forget the whole business.	**Puisqu'il en est ainsi [Dans ces circonstances-là] j'aime autant laisser tomber toute l'affaire.**

Examples **124-129** suggest that the best translation of an . . .*ing* construction may be found in a clause or a prepositional phrase.

130. A Frenchman listening to you would not understand a word you are saying.

Un Français qui vous écouterait ne comprendrait rien à ce que vous dites.

131. He looked worried, like a man expecting bad news.

Il avait l'air inquiet d'un homme qui s'attendrait à recevoir une mauvaise nouvelle.

For the use of the conditional in **130** and **131**, see the explanations following **50** and **193**.

132. He fired again, hitting the burglar in the left leg.

Il tira un second coup, qui atteignit le cambrioleur à la jambe gauche.

133. She took the first bus, getting off at 42nd Street.

Elle prit le premier autobus, et descendit à la 42e rue.

French avoids the present participle when the two actions reported are successive rather than simultaneous (**132, 133**).

H. English Past Participle

134. Closed on Mondays.

Fermé le lundi.

135. The Academy, founded in 1635, is concerned with revising the dictionary.

L'Académie, fondée en 1635, s'occupe de la révision du dictionnaire.

136. There is a registered letter for you at the post office.

Une lettre recommandée vous attend au bureau de poste.

137. Somewhat reassured, she continued.

Un peu rassurée, elle poursuivit.

138. His curiosity aroused, he moved cautiously toward the partly opened door.

Sa curiosité éveillée, il avança précautionneusement vers la porte entrebâillée.

139. Seen from a distance, the islands show no sign of human habitation.

Vues de loin, ces îles ne présentent aucun signe d'habitation humaine.

The English past participle used without an auxiliary verb may be considered as an adjective; and the French past participle, agreeing in gender and number with the noun or pronoun to which it refers, corresponds to it syntactically in the types of construction illustrated in **134-139**.

This does not mean that every independent past participle in the one language will be idiomatically translatable by a past participle in the other. For example, the equivalent of a sign in a restaurant window, *Waitresses and Dishwashers Wanted*, is **On demande serveuses et laveuses**; while the French **Entrée Interdite** becomes, in English, *No Admittance* or *Keep Out*.

140. A book sent to me by a colleague. . .

Un livre que m'a envoyé un collègue. . .

141.   This announcement, unexpected by
anyone, caused general dismay.

**Cette annonce, à laquelle personne ne
s'était attendu, provoqua une conster-
nation générale.**

Not infrequently, the English participial phrase is preferably, or necessarily, translated by a relative clause. The reverse is also possible. **Le père, jusqu'alors demeuré silencieux, prit soudain la parole** = *The father, who had said nothing until this moment, suddenly broke his silence.* See also **189-191.**

Section 2
BE AND HAVE

This section is made up of combinations in which:

1. the first element is any of the one-word forms of **BE** and **HAVE**, namely: *am, are, (to) be, being, had, has, (to) have, having, is, was, were* [*been* is never initial in a group]; and,

2. this form, singly or in combination with other forms of **BE** or **HAVE**, is followed *directly* by an infinitive, a past participle, or a present participle, and by no other relevant verb form. The "relevant" verbs are those marked with an asterisk in the index. (See paragraph II of Instructions for Use, page x.)

Thus, this section includes *had to leave, was killed, isn't working, are to arrive, was not to be sent, has been speaking, have had to be examined*, etc.

It does not include *WILL have arrived, are *going to explode, had* a house *built*.

The order of subdivisions is alphabetical by initial verb element, disregarding the word *to*.

BE . . .ed (For AM/ARE: see IS)

142.	They have ordered that he be put to death.	Ils ont décrété qu'il soit mis à mort.
143.	"Thy will be done."	«(Que) ta volonté soit faite.»
144.	It is imperative that this bill be passed as soon as possible.	Il est de toute urgence que ce projet de loi soit approuvé dans le plus bref délai.
145.	The manager insisted that we be given the best room in the hotel.	Le gérant insista pour qu'on nous donne la meilleure chambre de l'hôtel.
146.	Be seated.	Asseyez-vous.
147.	Be assured [Please believe] [You may be sure] that I will do everything I can to make your visit enjoyable.	Soyez persuadé [Soyez certain] que je ferai tout mon possible pour rendre votre séjour agréable.
148.	Be advised that we will take appropriate measures.	Sachez que nous prendrons des mesures de circonstance.
149.	Be seen there as much as possible.	Qu'on vous y voie le plus souvent possible.

Be + past participle, not preceded by *to* or by any auxiliary or modal, occurs only in the relatively uncommon present subjunctive passive (**142-145**) and the equally rare passive imperative (**146-149**). Literal translation is frequently possible for these subjunctives; it is usually not possible for the passive imperative, which almost always becomes active in French.

to BE . . .ed

150.	To be chosen Queen of the Festival, that was her dream.	**Etre nommée Reine de la Fête, c'était là son rêve.**
151.	His letter of application came too late to be considered.	**Sa lettre de candidature est arrivée trop tard pour être prise en considération [pour qu'on la prenne/prît en considération].**
152.	Not to be opened till Christmas.	**Ne pas ouvrir avant Noël.**
153.	Some packages to be delivered.	**Des colis à livrer.**
154.	She is waiting to be introduced.	**Elle attend qu'on la présente.**
155.	He was among the first to be rescued.	**Il était parmi les premiers sauvés [qu'on a sauvés].**
156.	There is little chance for them to be readmitted.	**a. Il y a peu de chances pour qu'ils soient réadmis.** **b. Ils ont peu de chances d'être réadmis.**
157.	The main thing is not to be caught.	**L'essentiel, c'est de ne pas se laisser attraper.**
158.	That was an evening to be remembered.	**C'était une soirée inoubliable [une soirée dont on gardera toujours le souvenir].**

The passive infinitive, not governed by an auxiliary or modal, is occasionally translatable by **être** + past participle (**150, 151**), but it is better translated by an active infinitive (**152, 153**) or by changing the construction in one of the ways suggested in **154-158**.

BE . . .ing

159.	Be talking about his book when he gets here.	**Soyez [Qu'il vous trouve] en train de parler de son livre quand il arrivera.**
160.	Be thinking about how we can sell them on our idea.	**Réfléchissez un peu sur les moyens dont nous pourrions leur faire accepter notre idée.**

The idiomatic *be thinking* of **160** is not truly a progressive form; it merely means *think* (in the near future) *a bit,* and this suggests a simple French equivalent.

to BE . . .ing

161.	He claims to be doing it for our own good.	Il prétend le faire dans notre intérêt.
162.	This is no time for us to be arguing among ourselves.	Ce n'est pas le moment de disputer entre nous.
163.	They pretended to be looking at the window display.	Ils affectaient de regarder dans la vitrine.
164.	It is advisable not to be yawning when the professor looks your way.	Evitez que le professeur (ne) vous surprenne en train de bâiller.

BEING . . .ed

165.	The door being closed, he could hear nothing at all.	La porte étant fermée [Comme la porte était fermée], il n'entendait rien du tout.
166.	Being [= The possibility of being] kicked out was the least of his worries.	a. La possibilité d'être expulsé ne l'inquiétait guère. b. Qu'on pût l'expulser, c'était là le moindre de ses soucis.
167.	A few days after being appointed treasurer, he disappeared.	Quelques jours après qu'on l'eut nommé [après avoir été nommé] trésorier, il disparut.
168.	She can't stand being interrupted.	Elle ne supporte pas qu'on lui coupe la parole.
169.	On being asked his name, he muttered something unintelligible.	Quand on lui demanda son nom, il marmonna quelque chose d'inintelligible.
170.	There is little hope of their being found innocent.	Il y a peu d'espoir qu'on les juge innocents.
171.	He did it without being told.	Il l'a fait sans qu'on lui ait [eût] dit de le faire.
172.	They were counting on their absence not being noticed.	Ils comptaient que leur absence ne serait pas remarquée.
173.	He was afraid of being gypped.	Il craignait d'être roulé.
174.	You have nothing to lose by being questioned.	Vous n'avez rien à perdre en vous laissant interroger.
175.	Avoid being left behind (in competition).	a. Ne vous laissez pas devancer. b. Prenez garde qu'on ne vous dépasse.

HAD . . .ed

176.	Someone had turned out the light.	Quelqu'un avait éteint la lumière.
177.	They had not yet taken out insurance.	Ils n'avaient pas encore contracté une assurance.

178.	She had been a librarian.	**Elle avait été bibliothécaire.**
179.	She had been a widow since 1965.	**Elle était veuve depuis 1965.**
180.	We had not been in Paris since the war.	**Nous n'avions pas été à Paris depuis la guerre.**
181.	I had not seen her for a long time.	**Je ne l'avais pas vue depuis longtemps.**

Example **178** is past perfect in both languages. But if, as in **179**, the English sentence indicates (often by a *for* or *since* phrase) how long a condition had been in effect or how long an action had been going on at a given time, French uses the imperfect with **depuis** to show continued duration at the past moment in question. In the negative, the past perfect is used (**180, 181**). See also **HAS BEEN . . .ing (263)** and **HAD BEEN . . .ing (213)**.

182.	If you had arrived a moment earlier, you would have seen them.	**a. Si vous étiez arrivé un instant plus tôt, vous les auriez vus.**
		b. Vous seriez arrivé un instant plus tôt, (que) vous les auriez vus.
183.	Even if I had put the bread in the refrigerator, it would be moldy now.	**a. Même si j'avais mis le pain dans le frigo, il serait moisi maintenant.**
		b. Quand même j'aurais mis. . .
		c. J'aurais mis. . . qu'il serait moisi (quand même).
184.	Had he not missed his two free throws, the game would have been sewed up.	**S'il n'avait pas manqué ses deux coups francs, le jeu était verrouillé.**

For an explanation of **était** in **184**, see note following **980**.

185.	When he had written it, he showed it to me.	**a. Quand il l'a eu écrit, il me l'a fait voir.**
		b. Quand il l'eut écrit, il me le fit voir.

The double compound tense (**passé surcomposé**) of **185a** translates *had . . .ed* in clauses beginning with **quand, lorsque, après que, dès que, aussitôt que,** and **à peine** when (1) the verb in the main clause is in the past indefinite, and (2) the sentence refers to a single sequence of events. The past anterior accompanies the past definite in the same pattern in formal style (**185b**).

The past perfect would be used after **quand** (etc.) only if the main verb were in the imperfect, denoting habitual or repeated occurrences. E.g., *When she had finished doing the dishes, her husband (would) put them away* = **Quand elle avait fini de faire la vaisselle, son mari la rangeait dans le buffet.**

186.	He said he would show it to me when he had written it.	**Il a dit qu'il me le ferait voir quand il l'aurait écrit.**

There is a time difference between the *when* clauses of **185** and **186** which is carefully marked in French. In **185**, the writing is clearly past with reference to another action which is also in the past. In **186**, the writing is future with respect to the promise, and past with respect to the showing, regardless of whether the latter action has already occurred or is yet to come. The conditional is used in French to refer to a *future in the past,* on the same principle as the one requiring the future tense in *when* clauses implying future time (see also 8 and 36).

187.	They brought him coffee although he hadn't asked for any.	**On lui apporta du café bien qu'il n'en eût pas demandé.**
188.	It was the first time she had had them to dinner.	**C'était la première fois qu'elle les recevait à dîner.**

The use of the imperfect in **188** shows that the reference is not to an event already past at the time of the main verb (**était**), but to a situation existing at that time.

189.	They were soldiers who had returned from Vietnam.	**C'étaient des soldats revenus du Viet-nam.**
190.	Her husband, who had gone hunting, would not be back till evening.	**Son mari, parti à la chasse, ne devait rentrer que le soir.**
191.	She gave away her dresses, which had become too small [for her].	**Elle a fait cadeau de ses robes, devenues trop petites.**

In connection with **189-191**, see the note to **44**.

192.	Had it not been for [But for] that traveling salesman who gave me a lift, I would still be out there on the highway.	**N'était [N'eût été] [Sans] le commis voyageur qui m'a pris à bord, je serais encore là-bas sur la (grande) route.**
193.	He looked like a man who had seen a ghost.	**Il avait l'air d'un homme qui aurait vu un revenant.**

The conditional (perfect) is used in **193** because the sentence does not state that a ghost has been seen, but rather that such an effect has come about as *would have* occurred *if* the person had seen a ghost. **Avait vu** in this clause would mean that the person's appearance was like that of an individual who had, in fact, experienced such a confrontation. Compare **50**.

HAD to

194.	I had to trust him; I had no choice.	**Il fallait bien me fier à lui; je n'avais pas le choix.**
195.	I realized what I had to do.	**Je comprenais ce que je devais faire [ce qu'il fallait faire] [ce que j'avais à faire].**
196.	We had to take a taxi.	**Nous avons dû prendre le taxi. [Il (nous) a fallu prendre...] [Il a fallu que nous prenions...].**
197.	They had to postpone their departure.	**Ils ont dû reculer leur départ.**

In **194** and **195**, the imperfect describes a past *state* of necessity or obligation; in **196** and **197** the past indefinite tells of a past *occurrence* of necessity, together with an implication that subsequent action has ended the matter.

198.	He had to make a delicate decision.	**Il eut [avait] à prendre une décision délicate.**

See note to **245.**

199.	It had to be George. Who else would be calling me up at 2 A.M.?	**C'était sûrement Georges. Qui d'autre me téléphonerait à deux heures du matin?**
200.	I guess it had to happen.	**Il était sans doute inévitable que cela arrive.**
201.	Then the old man had to butt in.	a. **Alors le malheur a voulu que le vieux s'en mêle.**
		b. **(Ne) voilà-t-il pas que le vieux s'en mêle.**

Had to in **201** is somewhat special; it does not refer to personal obligation or necessity, but rather conveys annoyance at capricious fate.

HAD to BE . . .ed

202.	She had to be dragged away.	**On a dû l'emmener de force.**
203.	The animal had to be destroyed.	**Il a fallu achever [tuer] la bête.**
204.	The exams had to be graded by Monday morning.	**Les examens devaient être corrigés avant lundi matin.**

HAD to BE . . .ing

205.	They had to be telling the truth. [= It is hard to imagine that they were not telling the truth.]	**Il était évident qu'ils disaient la vérité.**
206.	He had to be working; otherwise he wasn't happy.	a. **Il n'était content que lorsqu'il travaillait.**
		b. **Le travail était indispensable à son bonheur.**

Had to be . . .ing is probably best handled by mentally recasting the sentence in English. Another acceptable translation for **206, Il lui fallait travailler, sans quoi il s'ennuyait,** is structurally closer to the English, but quite informal.

HAD BEEN . . .ed

207.	The money had been deposited in a Swiss bank.	L'argent avait été déposé dans une banque suisse.
208.	They had been sentenced to five years of hard labor.	Ils avaient été [On les avait] condamnés à cinq ans de travaux forcés.
209.	Why hadn't she been notified?	a. Pourquoi ne l'avait-on pas prévenue?
		b. Pourquoi n'avait-elle pas été prévenue?
210.	If he had been [Had he been] brought up properly, he wouldn't be running around with such hoodlums.	S'il avait été élevé comme il faut, il ne fréquenterait pas des voyous de ce genre.
211.	Robert Kennedy, had he not been killed, might have won the Democratic nomination in 1968.	Robert Kennedy, s'il n'avait pas été tué, aurait pu remporter l'investiture démocrate en 1968.
212.	It was a problem that had not been encountered before.	C'était un problème qui se posait pour la première fois.

Although in **212** a literal **qui n'avait pas été rencontré auparavant** would violate no grammatical rule, the tendency in French would be to avoid so heavy a sequence of verbs in favor of a simpler construction which says the same thing.

HAD BEEN . . .ing

213.	We had been riding for more than an hour.	a. Nous roulions depuis plus d'une heure.
		b. Il y avait plus d'une heure que nous roulions.
214.	How long had he been living alone?	Depuis combien de temps vivait-il tout seul?
215.	He had been preparing a speech.	Il avait été en train de rédiger un discours.
216.	She had been visiting museums.	Elle avait visité des musées. [Elle avait passé le temps à visiter. . .] [Elle s'était amusée à visiter. . .]
217.	We had not been expecting that.	Nous ne nous y étions pas attendus.

When the English *had been . . .ing* (generally accompanied by a temporal phrase with *for* or *since*, or the expression *how long*) refers to a state or action existing at a past moment and initiated at some previous time, its French equivalent is the imperfect (**213, 214**). If *had been . . .ing* is not accompanied by an indication of duration, it is rendered approximately by the French past perfect (**216, 217**). The alternatives suggested for **216** are ways of expressing more precisely what may be implied in the English sentence. In **215**, the implication is *had been engaged in* or *had been in the process of.*

HAD HAD to

218.	He had had to yield.	a. Il avait dû s'incliner. b. Il lui avait fallu s'incliner. c. Il avait été obligé de s'incliner.
219.	If we had not had to wait in line at the ticket window, we wouldn't have missed the kickoff.	Si nous n'avions pas dû faire la queue devant le guichet, nous n'aurions pas manqué le coup d'envoi.

HAD to HAVE . . .ed

220.	To belong to the club, you had to have built your own boat.	Pour devenir membre du club, il fallait avoir construit soi-même son bateau.

HAS/HAVE . . .ed

221.	He has landed a good job out west.	Il a décroché un emploi intéressant dans l'ouest.
222.	We have had a rough day.	On a passé une rude journée.
223.	They have never gone out together.	Ils ne sont jamais sortis ensemble.
224.	Everything has gone according to plan.	Tout s'est passé selon les prévisions.
225.	She has been ill.	Elle a été malade.
226.	She has been ill for almost three weeks.	a. Elle est malade depuis bientôt trois semaines. b. Voilà bientôt trois semaines qu'elle est malade.
227.	How long have you worn those dirty trousers?	Depuis combien de temps portes-tu ce pantalon crotté?
228.	I have known him only since last fall.	Je ne le connais que depuis l'automne dernier.
229.	She has not been ill since childhood.	Elle n'a pas été malade depuis son enfance.
230.	I have not smoked for two months.	a. Je n'ai pas fumé depuis deux mois. b. Je ne fume plus depuis deux mois.

English present perfect is regularly translated by the French past indefinite (221-225), never by the past definite. But if the English verb, accompanied by *how long,* or by the words *for* or *since* plus an indication of time, refers to a condition *still in effect*, the French equivalent calls for the present tense with **depuis** or **voilà / il y a (226-228)**. In **230a**, the idea is *not once did I smoke during the last two months*—it is an *event* that did not happen. In **230b**, the emphasis is on the continuing *state* of abstinence. See also **HAS/(HAVE) BEEN . . .ing (263)**.

231.	It is the first time I have seen a ballet.	C'est la première fois que j'assiste au ballet.

Use of the present in translating **231** shows that reference is to an event still in progress, rather than to a completed action.

232.	If he has changed his mind, he hasn't told me (about it).	S'il a changé d'avis, il ne m'en a rien dit.
233.	When you have dialed the number, hang up.	Quand vous aurez composé le numéro, raccrochez.

Compare **233** with **8**. In both sentences, since the action is yet to be accomplished, French grammar requires a verb in the future; note that in the compound (perfect) tense of **233**, it is the auxiliary verb which marks futurity.

234.	Wait till I have finished!	Attendez (donc) que j'aie fini!
235.	I doubt that she has gone out in such weather.	Je doute qu'elle soit sortie par un temps pareil.
236.	"Has he sold his car?" "Yes, he has."	«A-t-il vendu sa voiture?» «Oui (il l'a vendue) (très avantageusement).»
237.	"Haven't you answered his letter?" "Of course I have."	«N'avez-vous pas répondu à sa lettre?» «Si! [Mais si!] (j'y ai répondu.)»
238.	You have read Gide, haven't you?	Vous avez lu Gide, n'est-ce pas?
239.	We have never been to the races, and neither has he.	Nous ne sommes jamais allés aux courses, (ni) lui non plus.
240.	She says she has never cut a class, but she has.	Elle dit qu'elle n'a jamais [Elle dit n'avoir jamais] séché un cours, mais elle se trompe. [. . ., mais ce n'est pas vrai.] [. . ., n'en croyez rien.]

It is meaningless in French to repeat the auxiliary verb alone as English does in **236-240**. Either the entire verb is repeated, often reinforced with additional words which make the repetition less apparent and less awkward **(236)**, or it is omitted altogether **(239)**. Example **240** suggests ways in which repetition can be avoided by rephrasing.

HAS/HAVE to (See also MUST and DOES NOT HAVE to)

241.	He has to file a claim within a week.	Il doit faire une réclamation en moins de [sous / dans un délai de] huit jours.
242.	You have to walk up; there isn't any elevator.	Il faut emprunter l'escalier [monter à pied], il n'y a pas d'ascenseur.
243.	Unfortunately, I have to take a year of chemistry.	Malheureusement, je suis obligé de faire une année de chimie.

244.	She hasn't been told what she has to do.	**On ne lui a pas expliqué ce qu'elle doit faire.**
245.	I have to have a word with you.	**J'ai [J'aurais] à vous parler.**

The student is cautioned against using **avoir à** indiscriminately as a substitute for **falloir** and **devoir,** the standard translations of *have to* in the sense of *must.* **Avoir à** usually implies the existence of some more or less tangible thing to be done, said, written, read, etc. In **245, J'ai à vous parler** implies *I have something to say to you* (compare with **J'ai quelque chose à vous dire**). The conditional **[J'aurais]** softens the assertion, implying *I would be glad of the opportunity to talk to you if you have a moment to spare,* or something of the sort.

246.	He doesn't work any harder than he has to.	**Il ne travaille pas plus qu'il ne faut.**
247.	The hottest afternoon of the summer, and the air conditioning has to be off.	**L'après-midi le plus chaud de l'été, (et) violà que la climatisation ne marche pas.**

Has to in **247** has an idiomatic and rather ironic quality; the sentence is not so much a statement of necessity as a complaint about bad luck. Compare **201.** (**Il faut** could also be used, with the same suggestion of resentment against malevolent forces.)

248.	I'm going to finish this report (even) if I have to stay up all night.	**Je suis décidé à finir ce rapport, même si je dois [dussé-je] [devrais-je] y passer la nuit.**
249.	This has to be our greatest victory ever! *(said of an event already a fact)*	**Ce triomphe est sans aucun doute le plus glorieux que nous ayons connu!**

Sentence **249** illustrates a relatively recent idiomatic extension of the meanings of *has to;* despite its dubious status in English grammar, its wide popularity demands that some French equivalent be offered.

HAS/HAVE to BE . . .ed

250.	The form has to be signed in the presence of a notary.	**Le formulaire doit être signé en présence d'un notaire.**
251.	You have to be recommended by three professors.	**Il faut être recommandé par trois professeurs.**
252.	They have to be shown how it works.	**Il faut leur en expliquer le fonctionnement.**

HAS/HAVE to BE . . .ing

253.	He has to be making five thousand a month to live on such a scale.	**Il doit gagner cinq mille dollars par mois pour mener si grand train.**

254.	I have to be typing when the boss comes in, or he thinks I have nothing to do.	Il faut que je sois en train de taper au moment où le patron arrive, autrement il croit que je n'ai rien à faire.

HAS/HAVE BEEN . . .ed

255.	He has been assigned to the intelligence section.	Il a été affecté au service des renseignements.
256.	The rehearsal has been called off.	a. La répétition a été décommandée. b. On a décommandé la répétition.
257.	Have these bottles been sterilized?	Est-ce que ces bouteilles ont été stérilisées?
258.	My question has not been answered.	a. Ma question n'a pas eu de réponse. b. Ma question reste sans réponse. c. On n'a pas répondu à ma question.
259.	We have been given additional privileges.	On nous a accordé des privilèges supplémentaires.
260.	How long have they been engaged?	Depuis combien de temps sont-ils fiancés?
261.	That has been known for a long time.	On sait cela depuis longtemps.

In connection with **255-259**, the student's attention is called to the remarks on the passive voice, *page xi*. For an explanation of the choice of tense in **260** and **261**, see note following **273**.

262.	How much will be left when all your debts have been paid?	Combien (vous) en restera-t-il quand toutes vos dettes auront été réglées?

See **233** and its accompanying note.

HAS/HAVE BEEN . . .ing

263.	We have been working at it for six months.	Nous y travaillons depuis six mois.
264.	Since when have you been taking those pills?	Depuis quand prenez-vous ces pilules?
265.	It has been raining quite a bit.	Il y a eu pas mal de pluie.
266.	She has been writing poetry.	a. Elle fait des vers depuis quelque temps. b. Elle a passé son temps à faire des vers. c. Elle s'est amusée à faire des vers.

The alternatives suggested for **266** are ways of expressing more precisely what may be implied in the English sentence. Compare **216**.

267.	That's what I have been wondering.	a. C'est ce que je me suis demandé.
		b. Voilà ce que je me demande (depuis quelque temps).
268.	We have been admiring your paintings.	Nous admirions [étions en train d'admirer] vos tableaux.
269.	I have been expecting you.	Je vous attendais.
270.	He has been complaining constantly.	Il n'a cessé de se plaindre.
271.	Haven't you been paying attention?	Vous n'avez donc pas fait attention?
272.	What has he been talking about?	a. De quoi parle-t-il?
	(the speech in question has not yet ended)	b. Qu'est-ce qu'il raconte?
273.	Lately he hasn't been playing well.	Il n'a pas bien joué dernièrement.

English *has been . . .ing* or *has been . . .ed,* if accompanied by the interrogative *how long* or the words *for* or *since* plus an indication of time, is rendered by the French **depuis** plus present tense. Otherwise, the English group has no exact counterpart in French. Most often, the past indefinite will come closest (**270, 271, 273**). Occasionally, a present tense is preferable, if the action or state is viewed as continuing (**267b, 272**). In **268** and **269**, the imperfect is in order; the English could also be *were admiring (when you came in)* and *was expecting.*

274.	He has been embezzling all this time? I can't believe it.	**Il aurait détourné des fonds pendant tout ce temps? Incroyable!**

(The conditional in **274**, as in **15**, reflects astonishment or disbelief.)

HAS/HAVE HAD to

275.	He has had to give up his plan.	a. Il a dû abandonner son projet.
		b. Il lui a fallu abandonner son projet.
		c. Il a fallu qu'il abandonne son projet.
		d. Il a été obligé d'abandonner son projet.
276.	She has never had to work.	a. Elle n'a jamais été obligée de travailler.
		b. Elle ne s'est jamais trouvée dans la nécessité de travailler.

HAS/HAVE HAD to BE . . .ed

277.	The rules have had to be revised.	a. Les règles ont dû être révisées.
		b. Il a fallu réviser les règles.
278.	He has not had to be told twice.	Il n'a pas été nécessaire de le lui dire deux fois.

HAS/HAVE to HAVE . . .ed

279. I have to have read it by tomorrow.
Je dois l'avoir lu [Il faut que je l'aie lu] pas plus tard que demain.

280. To be eligible, one has to have maintained a B average.
Pour être éligible, il faut avoir soutenu une note moyenne de B.

HAS/(HAVE) to HAVE BEEN . . .ed

281. To be valid, a contract has to have been signed by both parties.
Pour être valide, un contrat doit porter la signature des deux intéressés.

The English verb combination of **281**, hardly an indispensable one for the language, could be translated literally into **doit avoir été signé** without violation of grammatical rules; French usage, however, would tend to simplify the construction, either in the way suggested here, or by shortening it to **doit être signé** (which looks at the result rather than the action).

HAS/HAVE to HAVE BEEN . . .ing

282. The engine has to have been running for several minutes before the heater will work.
Le moteur doit être en marche depuis quelques minutes pour que le chauffage fonctionne.

HAVE . . .ed (See also HAS/HAVE . . .ed.)

283. Have done with it!
Finissez-en!

As an auxiliary verb with no corresponding third person *has* form, initial *have,* unless preceded by *to,* occurs with an immediately following past participle in no other expression than the idiom of **283**.

The type of passive imperative which has an unavoidable noun or pronoun between the two verb elements *(Have your bags packed by 6 A.M.)* is not included in this section. It is examined along with the causative construction (see **434**) which (in English) it resembles in structure if not in meaning.

to HAVE to

284. I am sorry to have to say this, but. . .
Je regrette la nécessité [qu'il soit nécessaire] de le dire, mais. . . [Je suis désolé de devoir le dire, mais. . .]

285. What a nuisance to have to lug all these books around!
Que c'est ennuyeux d'avoir à trimbaler tous ces bouquins!

286.	We are lucky not to have to eat here every day.	Heureusement (que) nous ne sommes pas obligés de manger ici tous les jours. [Il est heureux que nous ne soyons pas obligés. . . / Une chance que nous ne soyons pas forcés de. . .]

to HAVE . . .ed

287.	I am sorry to have disturbed you.	Je regrette [Je m'excuse] de vous avoir dérangé.
288.	They are sure to have left by now.	Ils sont sûrement partis à l'heure qu'il est.
289.	You are wise not to have argued. [= You were right not to argue.]	Vous avez eu raison de ne pas discuter.
290.	They are not likely to have taken along extra clothing.	Il est peu probable [Il est douteux] qu'ils aient emporté des vêtements de rechange.
291.	Pretend not to have noticed anything.	Ayez l'air de n'avoir rien remarqué.

to HAVE BEEN . . .ed

292.	He is glad to have been remembered.	Il est content qu'on se soit souvenu de lui.
293.	They are sure to have been observed.	a. Il est certain qu'on les a observés. b. Ils ont sûrement été observés.
294.	The captives are presumed to have been shot.	On présume que les captifs ont été fusillés.
295.	Is it a disgrace not to have been promoted?	Est-ce (donc) un déshonneur que de n'avoir pas été promu?
296.	To have been arrested for speeding is nothing to boast about.	Avoir été arrêté pour excès de vitesse, il n'y a pas là de quoi se vanter.

to HAVE BEEN . . .ing

297.	He claims to have been traveling at the time.	Il déclare avoir été en voyage à ce moment-là.
298.	Is it possible for the plane to have been flying so close to the ground that radar couldn't pick it up?	Est-il possible que l'avion ait volé [filé] à si basse altitude [ait rasé le sol de si près] que le radar ne pouvait le répérer?

HAVING to

299.	Having to take exams doesn't worry him, but he dislikes having to attend classes.	La nécessité de passer des examens ne l'inquiète pas, mais ça l'ennuie de devoir assister aux cours. [Qu'il doive passer des examens, ça ne l'inquiète pas. . . .] [Qu'il faille passer. . . .]
300.	You can have a good time without having to spend a lot of money.	On peut s'amuser sans qu'il soit nécessaire de dépenser beaucoup d'argent.
301.	He is afraid of having to defend his position.	Il craint d'être [de se trouver] obligé de justifier sa (prise de) position.
302.	I am surprised at his having to ask for our help.	Cela m'étonne qu'il doive chercher notre aide. [. . .qu'il ait besoin de chercher. . . .]
303.	He said something about having to consult his partner first.	Il a laissé entendre qu'il devait d'abord consulter son associé.

English *having to* is usually gerundive rather than participial, as **299-303** suggest. *Having to* does have a paradigmatic counterpart in **devant**, but **devant**, used participially, occurs mainly in contexts in which *since [he] had to. . .* is a smoother English translation. E.g., **Devant se rendre au bureau tous les matins, il. . .** is translated *Since he had to go to the office every morning, he. . .*

HAVING . . .ed

304.	Having lost my address book, I couldn't write to my friends.	Ayant perdu mon carnet d'adresses, je n'ai pas pu écrire à mes amis.
305.	He condemned the book without having read it.	Il a condamné le livre sans l'avoir lu.
306.	There is no excuse for having lied.	Il est inexcusable d'avoir menti.
307.	I am no better off for having taken his advice.	Je ne suis pas plus avancé pour avoir suivi ses conseils.
308.	They returned without his having noticed their absence.	Ils sont revenus sans qu'il se soit aperçu de leur absence.
309.	(After) having taken two aspirins, he felt better.	Ayant avalé deux cachets d'aspirine, il s'est senti mieux.
310.	(After) having taken two aspirins, he went to bed.	Après avoir avalé deux cachets d'aspirine, il s'est couché.

In **309**, the French present participle is used to show the suggested cause-effect relationship; in **310**, French **après** + perfect infinitive is used to indicate the merely temporal relationship of the two actions.

HAVING to BE . . .ed

311. You should put away your things without having to be told.

Tu devrais ranger tes affaires sans qu'on ait besoin de te le demander.

312. I found out only this morning about his having to be taken to the hospital.

C'est ce matin seulement qu'on m'a appris qu'il avait dû être transporté à l'hôpital [. . .qu'on avait dû le transporter. . . .]

HAVING BEEN . . .ed

313. The plants suffered no harm from having been left outdoors.

Les plantes n'ont pas souffert pour avoir été laissées dehors.

314. The meeting broke up without anything having been settled.

La séance fut levée [Le meeting se termina] sans qu'on eût rien résolu.

315. She was annoyed over not having been met.

Elle était vexée parce que [de ce que] personne n'était venu à sa rencontre.

316. Not having been told about the earlier starting time, we got there an hour late.

Ignorant qu'on devait commencer plus tôt que d'habitude, nous sommes arrivés une heure en retard.

317. Having been knocked down by cars twice before, he crossed streets very cautiously.

Comme il avait déjà été renversé [Ayant déjà été renversé] deux fois par des autos, il traversait les rues avec une extrême prudence.

318. Having been wounded in the leg, he couldn't walk.

Puisqu'il avait été blessé [Etant blessé / Ayant été blessé] à la jambe, il ne pouvait pas marcher.

319. That having been done, he went to dinner.

Cela fait, il alla dîner.

Word-for-word translation into French of *having been . . .ed* is impossible in such sentences as **316** (see remarks on the passive voice, page xi). Similarly, an **. . .ant** form is out of the question after the prepositions of **311-315**. Even when grammatically permissible, as in **317** and **318**, literal translation of *having been . . .ed* is clumsy and unnatural and should generally be avoided. In **319**, note that the English *having been* could even have been omitted entirely.

HAVING BEEN . . .ing

320. He denies having been drinking.

Il se défend d'avoir bu. [Il nie avoir bu.]

HAVING HAD to

321.	I regret your having had to change your plans.	Je regrette que vous ayez dû modifier vos plans.
322.	Never having had to cope with such a situation, he was at a loss what to do.	N'ayant jamais dû faire face à une situation pareille, il ne savait que faire. [Se trouvant pour la première fois dans une situation pareille. . . .]
323.	She admits having had to ask for directions before she got there.	Elle avoue avoir dû demander son chemin [s'enquérir de la route à suivre] avant d'y arriver.

IS/AM, ARE . . .ed

324.	There, it is done.	Voilà, c'est fait.
325.	They are caught in their own trap.	Ils sont pris dans leur propre piège.
326.	The last sentence is underlined.	La dernière phrase est soulignée.
327.	His name is spelled with an "x." (See note below)	a. Son nom s'écrit avec un «x.» b. Son nom est écrit avec un «x.»
328.	In France, coffee is not drunk with meals.	En France, le café ne se boit pas avec les repas.
329.	That is easily explained.	Cela s'explique facilement.
330.	The coal is transported by barge.	Le transport du charbon s'effectue au moyen de chalands.
331.	I am told (that) they don't ask to see your passport.	On me dit qu'il n'y a pas de contrôle des passeports.
332.	The mail is picked up at 9:30 a.m.	On vient prendre le courrier à 9 h. 30.
333.	Your attention is called to the fact [You are reminded] that cooking is not permitted in the rooms.	On vous fait remarquer [On vous rappelle] qu'il est défendu de cuisiner dans les chambres.
334.	Many are called; few are chosen.	Beaucoup sont appelés; peu sont élus.

Sentences of the type 324-326 tell the present condition or status of a thing or person—a condition which is actually the result of some completed action. The past participle is adjectival; compare *she is tired* = **elle est fatiguée.** Example 327b is comparable; note that it means something like *His name, in this particular instance, has been written with an 'x,' though it should be spelled with a* '**t**.' Translation 327a, using the present reflexive, denotes what is habitual, or, in this case, correct. Examples 328-330 further illustrate the French preference for the reflexive, rather than the passive, to express the habitual, the normal, the universal, as opposed to the temporary and the accidental. Sentences 331-333 exemplify the common use of **on** and an active verb to translate English passives when an unspecified personal agent is implied. **On** would not be used in 334 because there is no awareness of even a dimly identifiable personal agent.

IS/AM, ARE . . .ing

335. It is snowing in the mountains.   Il neige dans les montagnes.
336. You are wasting your breath.   Tu perds ta salive.
337. "Are they waiting for us?"   «Nous attendent-ils?»
      "No, they aren't."   «Non (ils ne nous attendent pas [ils
      (See note following 240)   sont déjà partis] [je ne crois pas],
                                                          etc.)»
338. She is ironing tablecloths.   Elle est en train de repasser des
                                                          nappes.

English *is . . .ing* has no exact counterpart in French. Do not attempt to translate it with a form of **être** + present participle. Example **338** is one way in which durative aspect can be expressed; others are found in **1208**. The relatively rare progressive **aller** + present participle (**Il va s'affaiblissant** = *He is growing weaker;* **La rivière va (en) s'élargissant** = *The river keeps getting wider*) is of limited application.

339. She is kneeling in front of the altar.
      a. [= She is in a kneeling position.]   a. **Elle est agenouillée devant l'autel.**
      b. [= She is (in the act of) taking a   b. **Elle s'agenouille devant l'autel.**
          kneeling position.]

See note following **123**. In French **339b**, the active form of the verb is used to mark action or change, as opposed to the static connotation of **339a**.

340. The train is leaving.   Le train va partir.

When *is . . .ing* refers to something on the verge of happening (compare *is about to. . .*), the French immediate future is a natural translation.

IS/AM, ARE to

341. He is to send us his reply by return   Il doit nous envoyer sa réponse par
      mail.   retour du courrier.
342. You are to stay here until everyone   Vous devez rester ici jusqu'à ce que
      has left.   tout le monde soit parti.
343. We are to look up his brother when we   Nous devons aller voir son frère quand
      are in Marseilles.   nous serons à Marseille.
344. She is not to leave the house for any   Elle ne doit quitter la maison sous
      reason.   aucun prétexte.
345. Am I to understand that he has gone   Dois-je [Faut-il] comprendre qu'il a
      bankrupt?   fait faillite?
346. You are to answer three of the four   On vous demande de répondre à trois
      questions.   questions sur les quatre proposées.

347.	You are to find two synonyms for each italicized word.	Il s'agit de trouver deux synonymes pour chaque mot en italique.

Is / am / are to, + active infinitive, is regularly translated by the present tense of **devoir**, never by a form of **être**. (See also **HAS to, MUST**, is *supposed to.) Examples 346 and 347, in which **devoir** could also be used, suggest idiomatic ways of translating these particular ideas.

IS/AM, ARE to BE . . .ed

348.	The dues are to be raised next month.	La cotisation doit [va] être augmentée le mois prochain.
349.	His statement is not to be taken literally.	Sa déclaration ne doit pas être prise au pied de la lettre.
350.	Nobody is to be let in without a ticket. *(instruction to door guard)*	Personne ne doit être admis sans billet.
351.	She is to be pitied.	Elle est à plaindre.
352.	He is not to be disturbed.	Il ne faut pas le déranger.
353.	He is not to be trusted.	On ne doit [peut] pas se fier à lui.
354.	He is not to be intimidated by threats.	On ne peut pas l'intimider [Il ne se laisse pas intimider] par des menaces.
355.	This bill is to be paid right away.	Il faut régler cette facture [Il faut que cette facture soit réglée] tout de suite.
356.	What is to be done?	a. Que faire?
		b. Qu'est-ce qu'on doit faire?
		c. Que faut-il faire?
		d. Que va-t-on faire?
357.	Where is such a man to be found?	Où trouver un tel homme?
358.	They are nowhere to be found.	On ne les trouve nulle part.
359.	Reference books are not to be taken from the reading room.	a. Les livres de référence sont à consulter [doivent être consultés] sur place.
		b. Les lecteurs sont priés de ne pas sortir les livres de référence.
360.	The aisles are to be kept free.	Ne pas encombrer les passages.

A fairly large number of examples have been given because of the variety of meanings covered by *is to be . . .ed*, which, in the affirmative, may express anything from mere futurity (348) to strict obligation (355), and in the negative has connotations ranging from mere advice or recommendation (349) to outright prohibition (352). The latter example also contrasts conspicuously in tone with 353 and 354, themselves dissimilar, although only the participle varies; French marks these differences by an assortment of modal auxiliaries. Examples 359 and 360 are included as further reminders that, in translation, the basic unit is not the word, but the idea.

In handling so idiomatic a combination as *is (not) to be . . .ed,* the student seeking guidance from this manual must be particularly careful to determine which of the models most closely parallels the thought he wishes to convey. Additional pertinent examples are to be found under **WAS/WERE to be . . .ed**.

IS/AM, ARE BEING . . .ed

361. Civilians are being evacuated.   **Les civils sont en train d'être évacués.**
362. The kitchen is being repainted.   **On est en train de repeindre la cuisine.**
363. He thinks he is not being paid enough.   **Il estime qu'il n'est pas suffisamment payé.**
364. Am I being asked my opinion?   **C'est mon avis qu'on demande?**
365. Are you being called for?   **Est-ce que quelqu'un doit venir vous chercher?**
366. No mail is being delivered today.   **Il n'y a pas de distribution de courrier aujourd'hui.**

IS/AM, ARE to HAVE . . .ed

367. By the end of the semester, we are to have read five novels.   **A la fin du semestre, nous devrons avoir lu cinq romans.**

IS/AM, ARE to HAVE BEEN . . .ed

368. At midnight all radios are to have been turned off.   **a. Il est défendu de faire [laisser] marcher les radios après minuit.**
b. Les radios doivent être fermées après minuit.
369. The finalists are to have been named by this evening.   **Les finalistes auront été nommés ce soir.**

WAS/WERE . . .ed

Before selecting a model from the examples below, the student is strongly advised to reread the note on the passive voice (page xi), especially the third paragraph.

370. The Eiffel Tower was erected in 1889.   **La Tour Eiffel fut édifiée en 1889.**
371. The play was banned in Boston.   **A Boston, cette pièce a été interdite par la censure.**
372. The power was shut off at ten o'clock.   **On a coupé l'électricité à dix heures.**
373. We were saved the trouble of making the trip.   **On nous a épargné la peine du déplacement.**

374. He was surrounded by admirers.
    a. *situation*
    b. *occurrence*
	a. **Il était entouré d'admirateurs.**
	b. **Il fut [a été] entouré par des admirateurs.**

375. The doors were draped in black for the occasion.	**Les portes étaient tendues de noir pour la circonstance.**
376. I was not surprised by the result.	**Le résultat ne m'a point étonné.**
377. Was anything said about the party?	**A-t-on parlé [A-t-il été question] de la surprise-partie?**
378. Was anything damaged?	**Y a-t-il eu des dégâts?**
379. She was not hurt in the accident.	**L'accident ne lui a causé aucun mal.**
380. He was carried away by his enthusiasm.	**Il s'est laissé entraîner [a été entraîné] par son enthousiasme.**
381. Three children were burned to death.	**Trois enfants périrent carbonisés.**
382. I wasn't born yesterday.	**Je ne suis pas né d'hier.**

WAS/WERE . . .ing

383. She was watering the flowers.	**Elle arrosait [était en train d'arroser] les fleurs.**
384. They were not looking in our direction.	**Ils ne regardaient pas de notre côté.**
385. He was standing behind the counter.	**Il se tenait [Il était debout] derrière le comptoir.**
386. He was leaning forward to hear better.	**Il était penché en avant pour mieux entendre.**

Was/were . . .ing cannot be translated by combining a form of **être** with a present participle. For the use of the past participle in **386,** see note following **123.**

WAS/WERE to

387. They were to bring all the necessary papers.	**Ils devaient apporter tous les documents nécessaires.**
388. She was to clean the stove and scour the pans.	**Elle devait décrasser la cuisinière et récurer les casseroles.**
389. What were we to think?	a. **Que fallait-il penser?** b. **Qu'est-ce que nous devions penser?**
390. You were not to say anything about it.	a. **Vous ne deviez pas en parler.** b. **On vous avait défendu d'en parler.**
391. Later, I was to realize he was right.	**Je devais comprendre plus tard qu'il avait eu raison.**
392. No one knew, of course, that this was to be his last game.	**On ignorait évidemment que ce match devait être le dernier de sa carrière.**

393.	What if they were to refuse?	a. Et s'ils refusaient?
		b. S'ils devaient refuser?
394.	(Even) if he were to offer me twice that much, I still wouldn't sell.	Il m'en offrirait le double que je ne le vendrais pas. [Même s'il devait offrir. . . / Dût-il offrir. . .]

Whether in the sense of *was supposed to, was expected to,* or *was destined to,* English *was to* is generally translatable by the imperfect of **devoir.** (See also **HAD to, WOULD.**) Examples **393** and **394,** in a somewhat different category, are to be compared with **38** and **847.**

WAS/WERE to BE . . .ed

395.	She was to be operated on the next day.	Elle devait être opérée le lendemain.
396.	The retrorockets were to be fired when the spacecraft was passing over the far side of the moon.	Les rétrofusées devaient être allumées pendant que le vaisseau survolait la face cachée de la lune.
397.	That was to be expected.	Il fallait s'y attendre. [On pouvait / aurait pu / devait / aurait dû s'y attendre.]

The wide choice of possibilities for translating **397** reflects the numerous shades of meaning attributable to the expression: *should have been. . ., could have been. . ., might have been,* etc. For further clarification, see these combinations in Section IV.

398.	That package was not to be opened.	Il ne fallait pas ouvrir ce paquet.
399.	The emergency exit was to be used only in case of fire.	On ne devait emprunter la sortie de secours qu'en cas d'incendie.
400.	He was not to be fooled so easily.	On ne le trompait pas si facilement. [Il ne se laissait pas tromper. . .]
401.	The committee decided that I was to be fined five dollars.	Le comité a décidé que je devais payer [de me faire payer] une amende de cinq dollars.
402.	Nothing was to be gained by waiting any longer.	Il était inutile d'attendre plus longtemps. [Nous n'avions rien à espérer en attendant. . .]

In addition to the above examples, examine the related constructions under **IS to BE . . .ed** (**348** and ff.), **IS to** (**341** ff.), and **WAS to** (**387** ff.).

WAS/WERE BEING . . .ed

403.	We were being followed.	a. Quelqu'un nous suivait.
		b. Nous étions suivis.

404.	I got there just as the curtain was being raised.	J'y suis arrivé juste au moment où le rideau se levait.
405.	She thought she was not being given enough freedom.	Elle jugeait qu'on ne lui accordait pas assez de liberté.
406.	Downtown, several old buildings were being razed to make way for the new city building.	Au centre, plusieurs vieux bâtiments étaient en train d'être démolis pour faire place à la nouvelle mairie.

WAS/WERE to HAVE . . .ed

407.	He was to have taken the seven o'clock train.	Il avaid dû [devait] prendre le train de sept heures.

If the seven o'clock departure is now a thing of the past, the expectation of leaving at that time is, strictly speaking, past perfect, (avait dû). But many speakers of English use *was to have (taken)* interchangeably with *was to (take)*; devait is then the French counterpart. The departure time may be in the past or the future with respect to the moment of the statement, which merely asserts a past expectation or intention. See also *supposed.

408.	They were not to have gone out without letting me know.	Ils ne devaient pas sortir sans m'en prévenir.

WAS/WERE to HAVE BEEN . . .ed

409.	The visitors were to have been taken to the White House by helicopter.	Les visiteurs devaient être transportés en hélicoptère jusqu'à la Maison Blanche.

Section 3

CAUSATIVES

This section comprises forms of the verbs **HAVE, MAKE**, and **GET**, combined with an infinitive or past participle plus one or more noun or pronoun objects, in their causative sense.

Note the following principles governing the grammatical objects involved in the **faire** causative construction:

1. If there is only one (noun or pronoun) object accompanying **faire** + infinitive, it is always a *direct* object. See for example **410, 411, 428, 429, 436, 444, 448, 454, 456, 457.**

2. When there are two objects, one is direct and the other must be either:

(a) an *indirect* object or

(b) a noun or stressed pronoun preceded by **par.**

See for example **414, 415, 430, 432, 435, 438, 447, 455, 464-467.** The direct object may be a noun *clause* (as in **469**).

3. The past participle of **faire** in the causative construction does not agree with a preceding direct object. See **422, 444,** and **466.**

GETS/GET (someone/something) . . .ed   (See also GET/GOT under Secondaries, Section 5)

410.	He gets his car washed every week.	**Il fait laver sa voiture toutes les semaines.**

The translation of **410** assumes that the meaning of the English is: *He arranges for [causes] his car to be washed.* In a conceivable context, it could mean that he is entitled to, or rewarded with, a weekly car wash, perhaps in return for some service on his part. Then of course it is no longer a causative, and French would say **(en retour) on lave sa voiture.**

411.	He gets it greased twice a year.	**Il la fait graisser deux fois par an.**
412.	Instead of throwing those shoes away, get them resoled.	**Plutôt que de jeter ces chaussures, faites-les ressemeler.**
413.	Get yourself introduced to the director.	**Faites-vous présenter au directeur.**

Distinguish between such sentences as the preceding, in which a second person actually performs the deed, and noncausatives of the type *She gets the dishes washed first thing* (= **Elle fait la vaisselle dès le repas fini**), *Get the engine started* (= **Mettez le moteur en marche**), in which an individual personally accomplishes an action.

GETS/GET (someone) to   (See also GET/GOT under Secondaries, Section 5)

414.	He gets his kids to clean the basement.	Il fait nettoyer le sous-sol par les gosses.
415.	He gets them to clean it.	Il le leur fait nettoyer.
416.	She gets people to listen to her.	Elle sait se faire écouter. [Elle se fait écouter.]
417.	Get the librarian to help you.	a. Faites-vous aider par le bibliothécaire. b. Demandez au bibliothécaire de vous aider.
418.	He is trying to get the chairman to recognize him.	Il cherche à se faire reconnaître par le président.
419.	He hopes to get the government to support his project.	Il cherche l'appui du gouvernement pour son projet. [Il voudrait / Il espère convaincre le gouvernement d'appuyer son projet.] [Il compte faire appuyer son projet par le gouvernement.]

GOT (someone/something) . . .ed   (See also GET/GOT under Secondaries, Section 5)

420.	He got his book published by a French firm.	Il a fait publier son livre par une maison d'édition française.

Do not confuse this use of *got* with its noncausative sense in *He got his book finished last week* (= **Il a achevé son livre**), in which no other person is mentioned as participating in the act.

421.	They got themselves hired.	Ils se sont fait embaucher.

GOT (someone) to

422.	She got her sister to drive her to the station.	a. Elle s'est fait conduire à la gare par sa sœur. b. Elle l'a fait conduire à la gare par sa sœur.

In **422a**, the person arranged the ride for herself; in **422b**, it was a third person who was given the transportation.

423.	They finally got him to admit it.	**Ils ont fini par le lui faire avouer.**
424.	I got her to sign them.	a. **Je les lui ai fait signer.**
		b. **Je l'ai persuadée de les signer.**

In **424a**, the equivalent of *I had her sign them,* no persuasion is implied, as there is in **424b**.

425.	We got him to hand over the key.	**Nous avons obtenu qu'il remette la clef.**
426.	She got her roommate to attend the lecture for her.	**Elle a persuadé sa compagne d'assister à la conférence à sa place.**
427.	She got three witnesses to testify in her behalf.	**Elle a trouvé trois personnes pour témoigner en sa faveur.**

In the last three examples we drift away from true causatives until, with **427**, we come to the idea of simply finding or obtaining someone or something. The French causative construction is correct in **422, 423,** and **424a**, would be ambiguous in **425**, extremely awkward in **426,** and quite impractical in **427**.

HAS/HAVE (someone/something) . . .ed

428.	The camp commander has all visitors searched before they come in.	**Le commandant du camp fait fouiller tous les visiteurs avant qu'ils n'entrent.**
429.	He has them searched.	**Il les fait fouiller.**
430.	She has breakfast served (to herself) in bed.	**Elle se fait servir le petit déjeuner au lit.**
431.	Have all those papers burned.	**Faites brûler tous ces papiers.**
432.	Have them brought to me.	a. **Faites-les-moi apporter.**
		b. **Qu'on me les apporte.**
433.	Ask to have them mailed to you.	**Demandez qu'on vous les fasse parvenir par la poste.**
434.	Have your shoelaces tied by the time I count ten.	**Que tes lacets de chaussure soient noués avant que j'aie compté jusqu'à dix.**

Example **434**, while not a causative, is included here for comparison. See notes following **283, 413,** and **420**.

HAS/HAVE (someone) [+ infinitive]

435.	He has the students repeat sentences.	**Il fait répéter des phrases aux [par les] étudiants.**

436.	She has us read aloud.	Elle nous fait lire à haute voix.
437.	Have them come in.	Faites-les entrer.
438.	Have her drink lots of fruit juice.	Faites-lui boire beaucoup de jus de fruits.
439.	Have her phone me at the office.	Demandez-lui de me téléphoner au bureau.
440.	Have them deliver it.	a. Faites-le livrer. b. Demandez-leur de le livrer.

Faites-le-leur livrer should not be used for **440**, since it means *Have it delivered to them.*

441.	She has her parents wake her up every morning.	Elle se fait réveiller tous les matins par ses parents.

HAD (someone/something) . . .ed

442.	I had several photographs taken.	J'ai fait faire plusieurs photographies.
443.	They had it sent to me.	Ils me l'ont fait envoyer.
444.	He had her thrown in jail.	Il l'a fait écrouer.
445.	We had a guard put around the house.	Nous avons fait surveiller la maison.
446.	I had my wallet stolen.	On m'a volé mon portefeuille. [Je me suis fait voler mon portefeuille.]

Note that English **446**, despite its syntactical similarity to the causative construction, does not really belong in the same category; the speaker did not arrange for the theft. Nevertheless, **faire** + infinitive is occasionally used this way, when there is no ambiguity.

HAD (someone) [+ infinitive]

447.	I had him fix the TV.	Je lui ai fait réparer la télé.
448.	They hardly ever had them recite.	On ne les faisait guère réciter.
449.	He had one of his assistants show us around the plant.	Il nous a fait visiter l'installation par un de ses aides.

HAS/HAVE HAD (someone/something) . . .ed

450.	She has had her face lifted.	Elle s'est fait retendre la peau du visage.
451.	They have never had the curtains cleaned.	Ils n'ont jamais fait nettoyer les rideaux.
452.	Have they ever had them dyed?	Les ont-ils jamais fait teindre?

MAKES/MAKE (oneself) . . .ed

453. They make themselves understood. **Ils se font comprendre.**

MAKES/MAKE (someone/something) [+ infinitive]

454. She makes them cry. **Elle les fait pleurer.**
455. She makes them empty the waste baskets. **Elle leur fait vider les corbeilles (à papier.)**
456. Nothing makes him change a decision once he has made it. **Rien ne le fait [Rien ne peut le faire] revenir sur une décision une fois prise.**
457. He makes coins disappear. **Il fait disparaître des pièces de monnaie.**
458. Those strawberries make my mouth water. **Ces fraises me font venir l'eau à la bouche.**
459. Make him write it over. **Faites-le-lui recopier.**
460. Try to make them accept it. **Essayez de le leur faire accepter.**
461. Make them obey you. **a. Faites-vous obéir.**
b. Insistez pour qu'ils vous obéissent.
462. Never make someone else do your work. **Ne faites jamais faire votre travail par un autre.**
463. She makes him go everywhere with her. **Elle l'oblige à l'accompagner partout.**
464. What makes you think so? **Qu'est-ce qui vous le fait penser?**

MADE (someone/something) [+ infinitive]

465. I made them peel the potatoes. **Je leur ai fait éplucher les pommes de terre.**
466. I made them peel them. **Je les leur ai fait éplucher.**
467. You made us miss our bus. **Tu nous as fait manquer l'autobus.**
468. His overacting made the audience laugh. **Son jeu exagéré fit rire les spectateurs. [. . .donna à rire aux spectateurs.]**
469. His answer made me realize I was wasting my time. **Sa réponse me fit comprendre que je perdais mon temps.**
470. They made him shave off his beard. **Ils l'ont forcé à couper sa barbe.**
471. He made me give it back to him. **Il m'a contraint à le lui rendre.**
472. What made you suspect him? **Qu'est-ce qui vous a amené à le soupçonner?**
473. He claims his prayers made it rain. **Il prétend que ses prières ont provoqué la pluie.**

As the above examples show, *made/make* (someone do something) is not invariably translated by the **faire** causative construction. The French equivalents of *oblige, force,* *persuade, induce,* etc., are alternates to be considered, and occasionally preferred for the sake of clarity. **Faire** + infinitive cannot be used in **471**, where there are three pronoun objects; and the causative construction is similarly impossible in **473,** because the impersonal **il** of **il pleut** cannot be put in the objective case.

PRIMARIES

In this text, the term *primaries* is used to designate auxiliaries and modal auxiliaries, exclusive of forms of **BE** and **HAVE**, which cannot be preceded in the same clause by any other verb form. They are: *can, could, does, did, let's, may, might, must, ought, shall, should, used to, will, won't,* and *would.*

The section also includes *do (don't)* as the finite form of the first two persons singular and the plural of the present tense, and *let (not)* as a third person imperative auxiliary.

CAN   (See also ABLE TO, Section 6)

474.	He can hold his breath for ninety seconds.	Il peut retenir son souffle pendant quatre-vingt-dix secondes.
475.	You can walk there in five minutes.	Vous pouvez y aller à pied en cinq minutes.
476.	Can I be of assistance?	Puis-je vous aider en quelque chose?
477.	She can read Greek.	Elle sait lire le grec.
478.	Now who can that be?	Qui est-ce que cela peut bien être?
479.	How can that be?	Comment cela se peut-il?
480.	What can I do about it?	Qu'y puis-je?

In general, **pouvoir** translates *can* when it is a question of physical ability (potentiality) or physical or moral freedom; **savoir** is used if it is a question of skill, training, or mental capacity.

481.	Write when you can.	Ecrivez quand vous (le) pourrez.
482.	Who can save him?	Qui pourra le sauver?

In **481** and **482**, future time is implied; compare **8** and **10**.

483.	You can see that I am busy.	Vous voyez bien que je suis occupé.
484.	I can understand your anxiety.	Je comprends bien que vous soyez inquiet.
485.	I can guess what his intentions are.	Je devine quelles sont ses intentions.

Though the standard translation of *can* is the present tense of **pouvoir,** idiomatic French frequently omits the modal in expressing the equivalent idea. This is characteristically true with verbs of physical or mental perception **(483-485).**

486. How can one make him understand that he isn't needed?	Comment lui faire comprendre qu'il est de trop?
487. There can be no doubt.	Il n'y a pas à douter.
488. I can hope, can't I?	a. Il est permis d'espérer, je crois. b. Il est permis d'espérer, n'est-ce pas?
489. He can leave when he wants to.	a. Il est libre de partir à son gré. b. Il peut partir quand il veut.
490. He doesn't answer. Can he be deaf?	Il ne répond pas. Est-ce qu'il serait sourd? [Serait-il donc sourd?]
491. Any number can play.	Le nombre de joueurs n'a pas d'importance.

Sentences in the above group illustrate a few of the French substitutes for **pouvoir.** More such variants will be suggested by the examples under **CANNOT, CAN BE . . .ed,** etc. Exploration of the French equivalents of *can* in all imaginable contexts would result in an unwieldy list of idioms, far exceeding the compass of this manual.

CAN NOT/CANNOT/CAN'T

492. He cannot do without coffee.	Il ne peut (pas) se passer de café.
493. Can't we meet in the conference room?	Ne pouvons-nous pas nous réunir dans la salle de colloque?
494. I can't get this spot out.	Je ne peux pas [Je n'arrive pas à] faire partir cette tache.
495. We can't just walk off and leave him.	Nous ne pouvons tout de même pas l'abandonner comme ça.
496. I can't help it.	Je n'y peux rien.
497. That cannot be (possible).	Cela ne se peut pas.
498. I can't tell you.	Je ne saurais vous le dire.
499. I can't find the switch.	Je ne trouve pas le commutateur.
500. I can't see myself as an actor.	Je ne me vois pas [Je me vois mal] en comédien.

As in the corresponding affirmative, **pouvoir** is commonly omitted in translating *cannot* with a verb denoting perception or an act associated with perception. Note, for that matter, the possibility of saying in English **(499** and **500):** *I don't find. . .* and *I don't see . . . .*

501. I can't complain.	a. Je n'ai pas à me plaindre. b. Il n'y a pas de quoi me plaindre. c. Je ne me plains pas.

The English of **501** is idiomatic; it is not a question of ability, but rather of having no reason to complain.

502. He can't be serious.
   a. [= He can't really mean it / He must be joking.]
   b. [= He is incapable of being serious.]

   a. Il doit plaisanter. [Pour sûr, il plaisante.]
   b. Il ne sait pas parler sérieusement.

503. He surely can't be afraid of us!

   Il ne se peut pas [Il n'est pas possible] qu'il nous craigne! [Il ne nous craint sûrement pas!]

504. You can't miss it. *(said by someone giving directions to a place)*

   Il n'y a pas à se tromper. [Vous ne pouvez pas vous tromper.]

505. One cannot (help) but admire [help admiring] his courage.

   On ne peut ne pas admirer son courage.

CAN BE . . .ed

506. The lid can be unscrewed.

   Le couvercle peut être dévissé. [Le couvercle se laisse dévisser / . . .se dévisse.]

507. They can be beaten.

   a. Ils peuvent être battus.
   b. Ils ne sont pas imbattables.

508. How can such conditions be tolerated?

   Comment (peut-on) tolérer [accepter] des conditions pareilles?

509. It can be expected that they will fight to the end.

   Il est à prévoir [On peut prévoir] qu'ils lutteront jusqu'au bout.

510. Tobacco can be obtained anywhere.

   Le tabac se vend partout.

511. Can the amount of fallout be controlled?

   Est-il possible de contrôler l'importance de la retombée (radioactive)?

512. You can be prosecuted for concealing stolen goods.

   Vous risquez de vous faire poursuivre (en justice) pour recel d'objets volés.

513. Nothing can be done about it.

   (Il n'y a) rien à faire.

Word-for-word translation of *can be . . .ed* is usually unidiomatic at best; the examples above suggest some common alternative construction, depending on the context.

CAN NOT/CANNOT/CAN'T BE . . .ed

514. The drawers cannot be locked.

   Les tiroirs ne peuvent pas être fermés à clef.

515. She cannot be reached by phone.

   Il est impossible [Pas moyen] de la joindre par téléphone.

516. The city hall can not be seen from here.

   D'ici on ne peut pas voir l'hôtel de ville.

517.	The theory cannot be proved.	Cette théorie n'est pas susceptible de vérification.
518.	It cannot be claimed that I showed partiality.	On ne saurait prétendre que j'aie montré de la partialité.
519.	Languages cannot be learned without effort.	Les langues ne s'apprennent pas sans peine.

Word-for-word translation of *cannot be . . .ed* is generally inadvisable and often impossible. Examples **515-519** illustrate some ways of handling the construction without using the passive voice.

CAN HAVE . . .ed

| 520. | Can he have swallowed that story? | Se peut-il qu'il ait avalé cette histoire? [Aurait-il avalé / A-t-il pu avaler / Peut-il avoir avalé. . .?] |
| 521. | How can they have overlooked so obvious an error? | Comment ont-ils pu laisser passer une erreur si évidente? [Comment une erreur si éclatante a-t-elle pu leur échapper?] |

The combination *can have . . .ed* is uncommon in English. Replaced in declarative sentences by *may have . . .ed* or *could have . . .ed*, it is used almost exclusively in interrogatives of the type shown; and even in these the popular preference is for *could have . . .ed*.

CANNOT/CAN'T HAVE . . .ed

| 522. | He can't have guessed what you were alluding to. | Il ne peut pas avoir saisi votre allusion. [Il n'aura pas pu saisir / Il n'a sûrement pas saisi votre allusion.] |

COULD   (See also ABLE, Section 6)

523.	She could get along if she had to.	Elle pourrait [saurait] se débrouiller au besoin.
524.	I'd clear out of here if I could.	Je décamperais si je le pouvais.
525.	You could at least be polite.	Tu pourrais au moins être poli.
526.	He could come and go as he pleased.	Il pouvait aller et venir comme bon lui semblait.
527.	How could you think he would forgive you?	Comment avez-vous pu croire qu'il vous pardonnerait?

The "standard" translations of *could,* as the equivalent of *would be able to* or *was/were able to* are, respectively, the conditional or the appropriate past tense of **pouvoir** (or **savoir**— see note following **480**). But do not overlook the examples below.

528.   Could he suspect something?
   a. [= Is it possible that he suspects. . .?]

   b. [= Was it possible that he suspected. . .?]

   a. **Se douterait-il de quelque chose?** [Peut-il se douter / Pourrait-il. . .?]

   b. **Se doutait-il de quelque chose?** [Pouvait-il se douter. . .?]

529.   How could he recognize you?
   a. [= How would he be able to. . .?]

   a. **Comment pourrait-il vous reconnaître?** [Comment vous reconnaîtrait-il?]

   b. [= How do you expect him to. . .?]

   b. **Comment voulez-vous qu'il vous reconnaisse** [puisse vous reconnaître] ?

   c. [= How did he manage to. . .?]
   d. [= How had he managed to. . .?]

   c. **Comment a-t-il pu vous reconnaître?**
   d. **Comment avait-il pu vous reconnaître?**

530.   He told me to call him as soon as I could leave the hospital.

   Il m'a dit de prendre contact dès que je pourrais quitter l'hôpital.

Compare **481**. **Pourrais** in **530** marks futurity with respect to the main verb, a standard use of the conditional.

531.   He could eat it all by himself.   **Il le mangerait à lui seul.**
532.   We could stand a bit of heat.   **On supporterait un peu de chauffage.**
533.   There is so much I could tell you!   **J'aurais tant de choses à vous dire!**
534.   I could kill him!   **Je le tuerais!**
535.   Why not ask him over for the weekend? He could sleep on the couch.   **Si nous l'invitions pour le weekend? Il coucherait sur le canapé.**

The idea of *could,* meaning something like *would, if given the opportunity,* is often expressed in French by the conditional of the English complementary infinitive, omitting **pouvoir** (531-535).

536.   How could he not be happy?   **Comment ne serait-il pas heureux?**

The meaning of **536** is not *How would he be able not to?* but *Why shouldn't he be happy (in view of the circumstances)?* or *How can/could one imagine his not being happy?*

537.   I could understand his hesitancy.   **Je comprenais son indécision.**
538.   He could see her silhouette against the light yellow drapes.   **Il voyait sa silhouette sur les rideaux jaune clair.**
539.   You could hear a pin drop.   **On entendrait voler une mouche.**

Could, followed by an infinitive such as *see, hear, imagine, understand,* etc., is often translated by the verb of physical or mental perception alone, since to state that one *could* perceive implies that one did (537, 538) or would (539) perceive.

540.	She thought she could talk him out of it.	Elle croyait pouvoir l'en dissuader.
541.	I could be mistaken.	Il se peut que je me trompe.
542.	I could be on the moon for all she cares.	Je serais dans la lune pour ce que cela lui fait.
543.	There could no longer be any doubt.	Il n'y avait plus à douter [plus de doute].

COULD NOT/COULDN'T

544.	She couldn't get up this morning.	Elle n'a pas pu se lever ce matin.
545.	He could not forget her.	Il ne pouvait pas l'oublier.
546.	It was no use, I couldn't lift it.	J'avais beau essayer, je ne pouvais pas [n'arrivais pas à] le soulever.

The distinction between past indefinite and imperfect holds for the verb **pouvoir** as for others. Differentiate between a statement to the effect that an event or action has proved impossible to realize (544), and a comment on a *state* of impossibility at a moment in the past (545). The choice of the imperfect in 546 underlines the condition of resistance or futility, as well as the duration of the effort. **Je n'ai pas pu le soulever** would be, in comparison, an unemotional report on the immovability of the object.

547.	Couldn't we rest for a while?	Ne pourrions-nous pas nous reposer un peu?
548.	If you didn't have a pass-out check, you couldn't get back in.	Sans la contremarque,
	a. [= ...you wouldn't be able (allowed) to get back in.]	a. vous ne pourriez pas rentrer.
	b. [= ...you weren't able (allowed) to get back in.]	b. vous ne pouviez pas rentrer.
549.	Would he say it if he couldn't prove it?	Est-ce qu'il le dirait s'il ne pouvait pas le prouver?
550.	I couldn't walk another step if my life depended on it.	Ma vie en dépendrait que je ne pourrais (pas) faire un pas de plus.
551.	That couldn't be true.	
	a. [= was not possibly true.]	a. Cela ne pouvait (pas) être vrai.
	b. [= cannot be true.]	b. Cela ne peut (pas) [ne saurait] être vrai.

Depending on context, *could not* may denote a real past (551a) or a softened assertion about the present (551b); this ambiguity disappears in French.

552. He couldn't understand why I had changed sides.	Il ne comprenait pas pourquoi j'avais changé de camp.
553. She couldn't get over it. *(She remained astonished, dismayed, incredulous, etc.)*	Elle n'en revenait pas.

COULD (NOT) BE . . .ed

554. No agreement could be reached.	Aucun accord n'a pu être réalisé.
555. He felt that a less expensive process could be developed.	Il était d'avis qu'un procédé moins coûteux pourrait/pouvait être mis au point.

Additional examples here would unnecessarily duplicate information already presented under **COULD, COULD NOT, CAN BE . . .ed**, and **CANNOT BE . . .ed.**

COULD BE . . .ing

556. They could be waiting for us in the lobby.	Ils nous attendent peut-être dans le hall.
557. He never talks to me about his work. He could be raising silkworms for all I know.	Il ne me parle jamais de son travail. Il élèverait des vers à soie pour autant que je sache.

COULD NOT BE . . .ing

558. Couldn't you be making better use of your free time?	Ne pourrais-tu (pas) mieux employer tes loisirs?

COULD HAVE . . .ed

559. They could have forged your signature.	Ils auraient pu contrefaire votre signature.

The variety of values assignable to *could* + compound infinitive in the absence of clarifying context makes it impossible to recommend an all-purpose equivalent in French. While the form suggested in **559** will be usable more often than not, the student should determine the precise meaning of *could have . . .ed* as he wishes to use it, and compare the examples below before selecting a translation.

560. He could have sold it.
   a. [= He may have sold it / Perhaps he has sold it / It is possible that he has sold it.]

   b. [= He would, in that case, have been able to sell it.]
   c. [= He had the possibility of selling it.]
   d. [= It was possible that he had sold it.]

a. **Il se peut qu'il l'ait vendu. [Il l'a peut-être vendu / il a pu le vendre / il aurait pu le vendre / il peut l'avoir vendu.]**

b. **Il aurait pu le vendre.**

c. **Il pouvait le vendre. [Il aurait pu le vendre.]**

d. **Il avait pu le vendre. [Il était possible qu'il l'eût vendu.]**

561. How could he have got [gotten] rid of it?
   a. [= How did he manage to get rid of it?]
   b. [= What possibility was there for him to get rid of it?]
   c. [= How had he been able (managed) to get rid of it / How was it possible for him to have got rid of it?]
   d. [= How would he have been able to. . .?]

a. **Comment a-t-il pu s'en débarrasser?**

b. **Comment pouvait-il s'en débarrasser?**

c. **Comment avait-il pu s'en débarrasser?**

d. **Comment aurait-il pu s'en débarrasser?**

562. You could have refused their offer.

Vous auriez pu [pouviez] refuser [ne pas accepter] leur offre.

563. You could at least have shaved.

Tu pouvais [aurais pu] te raser au moins.

564. If I had had some thread, I could have sewed that up for you.

Si j'avais eu du fil, j'aurais pu vous recoudre cela.

565. He would have enjoyed the play more if he could have understood it.

Il aurait pris plus de plaisir à la représentation s'il avait pu la comprendre [suivre].

566. Could he have taken the wrong road? *(See also 561)*

a. **Se serait-il trompé de chemin?**

b. **Pourrait-il s'être trompé de chemin?**

c. **Aurait / a / avait-il pu se tromper de chemin?**

567. Could she have copied somebody else's homework?

Est-il possible [Se peut-il] qu'elle ait copié le devoir d'un autre étudiant?

568. It hurt me to think that this man could have betrayed me.

Cela me faisait de la peine de penser que cet homme avait pu me trahir.

569. She could have been right.

Il se peut qu'elle ait eu raison.

570. I could have danced all night.

J'aurais dansé toute la nuit.

With **570**, compare **531-535**.

COULD NOT HAVE . . .ed

The remarks made in connection with **COULD HAVE . . .ed** are applicable here, and should be kept in mind when translating the negative. The bracketed possibilities in the examples below are not all free choices; selection must be based on the precise meaning and time value of *could not have . . .ed* as determined by context.

571.   They could not have prevented it.
    a. **Ils n'auraient pas pu l'empêcher.**
    b. **Ils ne pouvaient pas l'empêcher.**
    c. **Ils n'avaient pas pu l'empêcher.**

572.   You couldn't have pleased me more.
    Vous ne pouviez pas me faire plus grand plaisir. [Vous n'auriez pas pu. . .]

573.   He couldn't have spent that much money!
    Il ne saurait avoir dépensé tant d'argent. [Pas possible qu'il ait dépensé; il ne peut pas avoir dépensé; il n'aurait pas pu dépenser; il n'avait pas pu dépenser; il était impossible qu'il eût dépensé. . .]

574.   Couldn't they have climbed out the window? [= Isn't it true that they could have climbed out the window?]
    N'est-ce pas qu'ils auraient pu [pouvaient] [avaient pu] échapper par la fenêtre?

COULD HAVE BEEN . . .ed

575.   The program could have been prerecorded.
    a. **Le programme aurait pu être enregistré à l'avance.**
    b. **Il se peut que le programme ait été enregistré d'avance.**

576.   You could have been elected.
    Vous aviez des chances d'être élu. [Vous pouviez / auriez pu être élu.]

577.   You could have been killed.
    a. **Vous risquiez de vous faire tuer.**
    b. **Vous pouviez vous faire tuer.**

578.   They could have been thrown into the river.
    a. **Il se peut qu'on les ait jetés dans le fleuve. [On aurait pu les jeter . . .]**
    b. **Il est possible qu'on les ait jetés dans le fleuve.**
    c. **Il était possible qu'on les eût jetés dans le fleuve.**

COULD NOT HAVE BEEN . . .ed

579.   That sonnet could not have been
    Ce sonnet n'aurait pas pu être composé

written before 1620.   avant 1620. [Il est impossible que ce
                                        sonnet ait été composé. . .]

580. Couldn't the police have been notified?   **On ne pouvait donc pas avertir la
                                        police?**

COULD HAVE BEEN . . .ing

581. You should have knocked. I could   **Tu aurais dû frapper. J'aurais pu
      have been developing a film.   être en train de développer une
                                          pellicule.**

582. Who knows what they could have been   **Qui sait ce qu'ils pouvaient bien
      cooking up?   mijoter?**
583. He could have been trying to sound   **Il se peut qu'il ait voulu nous sonder.**
      us out.

COULD NOT HAVE BEEN . . .ing

584. She couldn't have been expecting you.   **Elle ne vous attendait sûrement pas.**
585. Couldn't he have been exaggerating a   **a. N'aurait-il pas exagéré un peu?**
      little?   **b. N'est-il pas possible qu'il ait
                                                  exagéré un peu?**

DID

586. Did you shut off the water?   **Avez-vous fermé l'eau?**
587. Did they pay you back?   **Vous ont-ils remboursé?**
588. Did he know you had resigned?   **Savait-il que vous aviez démissionné?**
589. What reason did she give?   **Quel motif [prétexte] a-t-elle
                                    invoqué?**
590. When did the repairman finally show up?   **Quand est-il arrivé finalement, le
                                                  dépanneur?**
591. How did she sprain her wrist?   **Comment s'est-elle foulé le poignet?**

The main role of *did*, as an auxiliary, is to combine with an infinitive to form interrogative or negative sentences in the past tense. The French equivalent of this unstressed *did* + infinitive is normally the past indefinite or, less commonly—chiefly with verbs of comprehending, knowing, believing, expecting, etc.—the imperfect (588).

592. He did find a key, but it isn't the   **Il a bien trouvé une clef, mais ce
      right one.   n'est pas la bonne.**
593. We weren't in Paris very long, but we   **Nous ne sommes restés que peu de
      did visit the Louvre.   temps à Paris, mais nous avons bien**

594.	You did put stamps on it, didn't you?	**Vous avez mis des timbres au moins?**
595.	"I *did* study!" *(said in answer to*	(Numerous translations of this reply
	"Why didn't you study?")	are available, depending on the

594.   You did put stamps on it, didn't you?   **Vous avez mis des timbres au moins?**

595.   "I *did* study!" *(said in answer to*   (Numerous translations of this reply
          "Why didn't you study?")   are available, depending on the
          emotional tone of the protest)

a. «**Ce n'est pas vrai que je n'aie pas
   étudié!**»
b. «**Qui vous dit que je n'ai pas
   étudié?** »
c. «**Comment, je n'aurais pas étudié?** »
d. «**Pas étudié?   Mais, je n'ai fait
   que cela!**»

596.   He said he would come, and he did.   **Il avait promis de venir, et il est
                                              venu en effet.**

597.   He didn't think he would succeed,   **Il n'avait pas pensé réussir, mais il
         but he did.**   a réussi tout de même.**

598.   He was planning to leave, but we   **Il comptait partir, mais nous ne savons
         don't know if he did (or not).**   pas s'il est parti ou non [. . .s'il est
                                              vraiment parti].**

599.   We played golf yesterday. Did *you*?   **Nous, on a joué au golf hier. Et vous?**

600.   "We played golf yesterday."   «**Nous avons joué au golf hier.**»
         "*Did* you?"   «**Ah, bon?** » [**Tiens!**] [**Sans blague?**]

The question in **600** is not so much a genuine inquiry as a polite way of showing that one is interested in, or at least has been listening to, what the other person has said.

601.   "Didn't they invite you?"   «**On ne vous a pas invité?** »
         "Of course they did!"   «**(Mais) bien sûr qu'on m'a invité!**»
602.   I drank more of it than he did.   **J'en ai absorbé plus que lui.**

Stressed *did,* plus infinitive to convey insistence (**592-595**) or standing alone as replacement for an antecedent verb (**596-602**), has no counterpart in the French verb system. Emphatic *did* can often be translated by an adverb–most commonly, **bien.** Sometimes it is advisable to recast the idea. In any case, the French auxiliary cannot stand alone; the verb is either omitted altogether or repeated in its entirety, generally reinforced with additional words which receive the stress and make the repetition less obvious (**596-598**).

603.   He told me to wake him up, and now   **Il m'avait dit de le réveiller, et
         he's mad because I did.**   voilà qu'il m'en veut de l'avoir fait
                                              [. . .parce que je l'ai fait].**

604.   I travel more than my father did.   **Je voyage plus que ne faisait mon
                                              père.**

Faire sometimes serves as a verb of replacement, notably in clauses of comparison (**604**), or in reference to some specific *deed* (**603**), where the verb has its primary sense of *to do* or *to make*. It could not be used in **592-602**.

DID NOT / DIDN'T

605.	He didn't charge us for the wine. *(= neglected to put it on the bill)*	**Il ne nous a pas compté le vin.**
606.	It was obvious that he didn't share our opinion.	**Il était évident qu'il ne partageait pas notre avis.**
607.	If the color didn't suit you, why didn't you exchange it?	**Si la couleur ne vous plaisait pas, pourquoi ne l'avez-vous pas échangé?**

The above are the standard equivalent tenses (see note following **591**). But consider the examples below.

608.	Oh, excuse me, I didn't see you.	**Oh, pardon, je ne vous avais pas vu.**
609.	Didn't I tell you he would louse up the job?	**Ne vous avais-je pas dit qu'il gâcherait le besogne? [Quand je vous disais. . .?]**

French frequently is more precise than English in the choice of tense. What is meant in **608**, and is shown by the French pluperfect, is that the speaker, who *has now seen* the other person, *had not yet seen* him at the moment of doing something he presumably would not have done if aware of the other's presence. In **609**, the telling obviously took place before the predicted occurrence, which itself is now past. The bracketed alternative is idiomatic; the imperfect here seems to connote reproach *(Why didn't you listen to me?)* or exultation *(There! You see? I was right and you were wrong.)*.

610.	He thinks he made a good impression, but he didn't.	**Il croit avoir fait bonne impression, mais il se trompe [. . .mais c'est plutôt le contraire].**
611.	"You swiped my matches!" "I did not!"	**«T'as fauché mes allumettes!» «Ah, pardon! C'est pas moi!»**

Didn't, standing by itself in replacement of a preceding verb, is often best handled in French by substituting some other expression which, in the context, carries approximately the same meaning as would the negated antecedent (**610**). See also **596-602** and accompanying note. As for the *I did not!* of **611**, the proposed translation is only one—the most restrained!— of countless conceivable rejoinders, whose phrasing and duration would vary with the relationship of the two individuals, the **esprit** of the accused, and the degree of warmth or feigned warmth engendered by the charge.

DID HAVE to   (See also HAD to)

612.	Did you have to go very far to get milk?	Tu as dû aller loin pour avoir du lait?
613.	No, but I did have to wait for the store to open.	Non, j'ai dû pourtant attendre que la laiterie soit ouverte. [Non, mais j'ai dû attendre . . . .]

DID NOT HAVE to

614.	He did not have to explain.	a. Il n'a pas été [n'était pas] obligé de s'expliquer. b. On ne lui a pas demandé de s'expliquer.
615.	We did not have to look very long.	Nous n'avons pas eu à chercher longtemps.
616.	She did not have to speak French to be understood.	Elle n'a pas eu besoin de [n'a pas trouvé nécessaire de] [n'a pas dû] parler français pour se faire comprendre.

The above are typical and unambiguous ways of expressing absence of necessity or obligation in the past. Compare:

617.	Didn't you have to show your identification card?	N'a-t-il pas fallu présenter votre carte d'identité?

In **617 falloir** may be used because, in contrast to **614-616**, where necessity is denied, the sentence implies the speaker's supposition of necessity. The expressions suggested for **614-616** would, of course, be usable in **617** as well.

DID NOT HAVE to BE . . .ed

618.	Fortunately, the seating capacity did not have to be increased.	Heureusement, le nombre de places n'a pas dû être augmenté. [Il n'a pas été nécessaire d'augmenter le nombre . . . .]

DO / DOES

619.	Do Japanese children play marbles?	Les petits Japonais jouent-ils aux billes?
620.	Does the ship roll much?	Est-ce que le bateau roule beaucoup?

621.   (How) do you like your room?   Êtes-vous content de votre chambre?

The principal role of *do/does*, as an auxiliary, is to combine with an infinitive to form interrogative (and negative—see **DO NOT/DOES NOT**) sentences in the present tense. The corresponding constructions in French do not require an auxiliary verb.

622.   Do be quiet!   **Tais-toi donc!**
623.   Do help yourself!   **Servez-vous, je vous (en) prie.**
624.   Do bring the children!   **Amenez les enfants, je le veux.**
625.   Do come and see us!   **Ne manquez pas de venir nous voir.**

Since French lacks an auxiliary verb corresponding to *do*, the insistent imperative must be rendered by means of a reinforcing adverb, an appendant clause, or a rephrasing of the command (**622-625**).

626.   Yes, he does seem tired.   **Oui, il a l'air fatigué, en effet.**
627.   Why, I do believe you are blushing!   **Mais, je crois bien [on dirait bien]**
                                              que vous rougissez.
628.   I do want to attend; it's just that   **Je voudrais vraiment y assister; c'est**
       I'm swamped with work.   **que je suis débordé de boulot.**
629.   He seldom leaves the house, but he   **Il ne sort que rarement; il va toutefois**
       does take in a movie now and then.   **de temps en temps au cinéma.**

For want of a French counterpart, the auxiliary *does/do*, when stressed, is commonly translated adverbially (**626-629**).

630.   She does ride a bicycle—I've seen her. **Pas de doute qu'elle se promène à**
                                              bicyclette—je l'ai vue (faire).
631.   He may not be much of a lecturer,   **(C'est un) conférencier assez médiocre**
       but he does know his classics.   **si vous voulez, mais il faut convenir**
                                              qu'il possède les classiques. [. . .mais
                                              il est incontestable qu'il possède . . . . /
                                              on ne peut pas nier qu'il possède . . . .]

Another solution to the problem of insistent *does/do* plus infinitive is to subordinate the verb in question to some appropriate stressable expression (**630, 631**).

632.   "Do you swear to abide by the rules   **«Jurez-vous de vous conformer aux**
       and regulations of the society?"   **statuts et règlements de la société? »**
       "I do."   **«Je le jure.»**
633.   I don't smoke, but my wife does.   **Moi, je ne fume pas; (mais) ma femme,**
                                              si. [. . .mais ma femme aime bien les
                                              cigarettes.] [. . .fume de temps en
                                              temps.] [. . .fume comme un sapeur.]
634.   "He phones his mother every day."   **«Il téléphone à sa mère tous les jours.»**
       "Who does?"   **«Qui ça? »**

635.	"Surely the ride won't cost over a dollar."	«Le trajet ne coûtera sûrement pas plus d'un dollar.»
	"But what if it does?"	«Et si ton pronostic s'avère faux?» [Et s'il coûte plus cher quand même?]
636.	"Would you like me to take you there?"	«Voulez-vous que je vous y conduise?»
	"Please do."	«S'il vous plaît.»
637.	"Shall I bring my tape recorder?"	«Dois-je apporter mon magnétophone?»
	"Yes, do! (by all means)!"	«Oui, surtout!»
638.	"I feel like taking a nap."	«J'ai envie de faire un somme.»
	"Then do so!"	«Alors, ne vous gênez pas!»
639.	I'll probably get to Brussels before he does.	Il est probable que je gagnerai Bruxelles avant lui.

Examples **632-639** illustrate how French might handle, in various contexts, the translation of *does/do* as a verb of replacement. Repetition of the antecedent verb is considered to be poor style; when the verb is reused, the expression is almost always rounded out with additional words which assume the stress and make the repetition less noticeable (**633**, last two bracketed examples). In formal situations, unembellished repetition of the first verb may be in order (**632**).

DO NOT (DON'T) / DOES NOT (DOESN'T)   (See also DO/DOES, DID, and DID NOT)

640.	Don't eat so fast.	Ne mange [mangez] pas si vite.
641.	Don't give me a bad time.	Ne me compliquez pas la vie.
642.	Don't kid yourself.	Ne te fais pas d'illusions.
643.	That does not concern me.	Cela ne me regarde pas.
644.	Doesn't he know what's going on?	Ne sait-il (donc) pas ce qui se passe?
645.	I don't guarantee to be there at eight o'clock.	Je ne réponds pas d'être là à huit heures.
646.	Do not confuse *"Provence"* and *"province."*	Ne pas confondre «Provence» et «province.»
647.	Do not lean out.	Ne pas se pencher au dehors.

General commands, warnings, and instructions are often expressed by the infinitive (**646, 647**).

648.	Don't think that I doubt your sincerity.	N'allez pas croire que je doute de votre bonne foi.

The admonition of **648** has approximately the value of *Now don't [on that account] [for a moment] [whatever you do] get the notion that* . . . .

649.	Why don't we ever eat out?	Comment se fait-il qu'on ne dîne?

		jamais au restaurant [en ville]?
		[Pourquoi est-ce qu'on ne dîne jamais. . .?]
650.	Why don't we eat out tonight?	Si nous dînions au restaurant ce soir?

In contrast to **649**, the English question in **650** does not ask for an explanation, but idiomatically proposes an idea; it is another way of saying *What say we eat out?*

651.	He says he works for the university, but he doesn't.	Il prétend être employé de l'université; n'en croyez rien.
652.	She'll manage. At least, I'll be surprised if she doesn't.	Elle saura se débrouiller. Du moins, le contraire m'étonnerait.
653.	I think it's time to begin. Don't you?	Je crois qu'il est [serait] temps de commencer. D'accord?
654.	He thinks I don't like him—and I don't.	Il a dans l'idée que je ne l'aime pas, et il a raison (de le croire). [. . .en quoi il ne se trompe pas.]
655.	My husband likes snails, but I don't.	Mon mari aime les escargots; moi, je les déteste. [. . .moi, non.]
656.	Why shouldn't he play poker if he wants to? You play bridge, don't you?	Pourquoi ne jouerait-il (pas) au poker si ça lui plaît? Vous jouez bien au bridge, vous!

Examples **651-656** show various ways in which French, lacking an auxiliary verb to handle the functions of *do*, might translate the negative forms of this verb of replacement. For further possibilities, compare **596-604, 610, 633-639**.

657.	He'll probably get well, but what if he doesn't?	Il est probable qu'il guérira, mais s'il ne guérit pas?

Repetition of the antecedent verb, to be avoided in affirmative sentences of this kind (see note following **639**), is less objectionable in the negative because **pas,** like the adverbial expressions **de temps en temps** and **quand même** of **633** and **635**, draws the stress to itself.

658.	France does not want to be drawn into a conflict which she does not approve.	La France ne veut pas être entraînée dans un conflit qu'elle n'approuverait pas.

Approval or non-approval can only be "conditional," in French, as long as the potential conflict is of uncertain nature. The indicative **approuve** would imply a specific or existing conflict on which the country has already taken a position. Note that the English could also read *may [might] not approve.*

DO NOT (DON'T) BE . . .ed

659.	Don't be frightened.	N'ayez pas peur.

660. Don't be tempted to sneak out. — Résistez à la tentation de sortir à la dérobée. [Gardez-vous de sortir . . . .]

661. Don't be seen in that neighborhood. — Qu'on ne vous voie pas dans ce quartier-là. [Il ne faut pas qu'on vous voie . . . .]

662. Don't be misled by deceptive advertising. — Ne vous laissez pas tromper par une publicité mensongère.

The only conceivable occurrence of *do not be . . .ed* is the negative-imperative-passive (or negative-imperative + adjectival past participle [**659**]). Its best equivalents in French are either an active imperative (second person) which says the same thing in another way, a third person active imperative (= subjunctive), or the construction using **laisser** (sometimes **faire**) + infinitive.

DO NOT (DON'T) BE . . .ing

663. Don't be doing crosswords when the boss comes in. — Ne soyez pas en train de faire des mots croisés quand le patron arrivera.

DO/DOES HAVE to   (See also HAS to)

664. Do we have to remember all those figures? — Faut-il retenir [Faut-il que nous retenions] tous ces chiffres? [Est-il indispensable de retenir. . .?]

665. Why does she have to be so unpleasant? — Pourquoi faut-il qu'elle soit si désagréable?

DO NOT/DOES NOT HAVE to

666. He doesn't have to work for a living. — Il n'est pas obligé [Il n'a pas besoin] de (travailler pour) gagner son pain.

667. We don't have to spend any time here if you'd rather move on. — Rien ne nous contraint à nous attarder ici si tu préfères continuer.

668. It doesn't have to happen that way. — Cela ne se passera pas forcément comme ça.

669. Don't you have to be twenty-one to vote? *(Compare 616)* — Ne faut-il pas avoir vingt et un ans pour voter?

670. Why take math if you don't have to? — Pourquoi faire des maths puisque ce n'est pas obligatoire?

671. You don't have to be crazy to work here, but it helps. — Il n'est pas nécessaire d'être fou pour travailler ici, mais ça vaut mieux.

DO/DOES HAVE to BE . . .ed

672.	Do you have to be told twice?	Faut-il vous le répéter?
673.	Does the ticket have to be validated?	a. Est-ce que le billet doit être validé?
		b. Faut-il faire valider le billet?
674.	Do the pages have to be numbered?	Faut-il que les pages soient numérotées?

DO NOT/DOES NOT HAVE to BE . . .ed

675.	This radio runs on batteries; it doesn't have to be plugged in.	Ce poste marche sur piles; on n'a pas besoin de le brancher.
676.	These shirts don't have to be ironed.	Il n'est pas nécessaire de (faire) repasser ces chemises.

LET'S/LET (not)

677.	Let's see how it looks.	Voyons comment ça se présente.
678.	Let's forget about it.	a. N'en parlons plus.
		b. N'y pensons plus.
679.	Let us not overlook any clue.	Ne négligeons aucun indice.
680.	Let r be the radius of any circle.	Soit r le rayon d'un cercle quelconque.
681.	Let there be no misunderstanding!	Qu'on ne s'y méprenne pas!
682.	Let him borrow money from somebody else.	Qu'il s'adresse à quelqu'un d'autre pour emprunter de l'argent.

Let's + infinitive is rendered by the first person plural imperative. So is the more formal *let us*, meaning the same thing. (For *let us* in the sense of *permit us to*, see **1063**.) *Let* in **681** and **682** is the sign of the English third person imperative, handled by the subjunctive in French.

MAY

683.	An elephant may live a hundred years.	Un éléphant peut vivre cent ans.
684.	"She may prefer jewelry."	«Il se peut qu'elle préfère un bijou.»
	"Yes, she may (at that)."	[Elle peut/pourrait préférer. . .]
		«Oui, ça se peut.» [Oui, c'est vrai.]
685.	May I say something?	Puis-je dire deux mots?
686.	May I? (have one / borrow this / sit here / etc.)	Vous permettez?
687.	You may be satisfied, but he isn't.	Vous êtes peut-être satisfait, mais lui ne l'est pas.

688.	You may leave (if you wish).	a. **Vous êtes libre de partir.**
		b. **Vous pouvez partir.**
689.	I am afraid the task may be too much for him.	**J'ai peur que la tâche ne soit au-dessus de ses forces.**
690.	So that everyone may know what the problem is. . .	**Pour que chacun sache bien de quoi il s'agit. . .**
691.	The probability, however slight it may be, is still there.	**La probabilité, si faible soit-elle, existe.**
692.	Come what may.	**Quoi qu'il arrive.**
693.	Be that as it may.	**Quoi qu'il en soit.**
694.	May he never regret it!	**Puisse-t-il ne jamais le regretter!**
695.	Much good may it do him!	**Grand bien lui fasse!**
696.	We may as well shoot the works.	**Autant vaudrait risquer le paquet.**

May, in its usual meanings as an expression of possibility or permission, corresponds generally to the present tense of **pouvoir**. The introductory **il se peut que** (= *it is possible that*) and the adverbial **peut-être (684, 687)** are usually dependable ways of handling the idea of *may* in the former sense. The English modal is sometimes used in a formally phrased (**694**) or sarcastic (**695**) expression of a wish. It is occasionally an optional translation of a French subjunctive: in **689** *may be* is an attenuated *is*; in **690** *may know* is roughly equivalent to *will know*. Finally, *may* is found in the approximate counterpart of various idiomatic expressions.

MAY NOT

697.	She may not listen to you.	a. **Elle ne vous écoutera peut-être pas.**
		b. **Il est possible / il se peut qu'elle ne vous écoute pas.**
698.	Minors may not vote.	**Les mineurs n'ont pas le droit de voter.**
699.	No, you may *not* have two desserts.	**Non, tu n'auras pas deux desserts.**
700.	This may not be the liveliest town in the world, but there is still plenty to do.	**Que cette ville ne soit pas la plus animée du monde, je ne le nie pas, mais elle offre tout de même pas mal de distractions. [Cette ville n'est peut-être pas. . ., (je ne dis pas le contraire. . .)]**

MAY BE . . .ed

701.	Boats may be rented by the hour or the day.	**Les bateaux peuvent être loués à l'heure ou à la journée.**

702.   They may be stuck in the traffic somewhere.

Ils sont peut-être coincés dans un embouteillage. [Il se peut qu'ils soient pris. . .]

MAY NOT BE . . .ed

703.   Your plan may not be approved.

Votre projet peut n'être pas approuvé. [. . .risque de n'être pas approuvé.] [Il se peut que / il y a des chances pour que votre plan ne soit pas approuvé.]

704.   Notebooks may not be taken into the examination room.

Les cahiers ne doivent pas être apportés dans la salle des examens. [Il est interdit d'apporter. . .]

MAY BE . . .ing

705.   She may be concocting some new dish.

Elle est peut-être en train de confectionner quelque plat nouveau. [Elle est peut-être à confectionner. . .]

706.   He may not be getting enough exercise.

C'est peut-être qu'il ne prend pas assez d'exercice.

The «c'est. . .que» of 706 is a standard device to introduce an explanatory remark in continuation of a discussion already begun.

MAY BE ABLE to

707.   We may be able to combine business with pleasure.

Nous pourrons peut-être joindre l'utile à l'agréable.

MAY NOT BE ABLE to

708.   I may not be able to get away from the office at noon.

Je ne pourrai peut-être pas m'absenter du bureau à midi.

MAY HAVE to

709.   They may have to break down the door.

Ils seront peut-être obligés de défoncer la porte.

MAY NOT HAVE to

710. You may not have to move out right away.

Il est (fort) possible que vous n'ayez pas à déménager tout de suite. [Vous ne devrez peut-être pas déménager. . .]

MAY HAVE . . .ed

711. She may have gone out.

a. Il se peut qu'elle soit sortie.
b. Elle est peut-être sortie.
c. Elle a pu sortir.

712. Your enthusiasm may have inspired his.

Votre enthousiasme a pu éveiller le sien.

713. Don't believe everything you may have heard.

Ne croyez pas tout ce que vous avez pu entendre.

MAY NOT HAVE . . .

714. They may not have seen us come in.

a. Ils ne nous ont peut-être pas vus entrer.
b. Il se peut qu'ils ne nous aient pas vus entrer.

MAY NOT HAVE . . .ed

715. She may have been overcome by the excitement.

Elle a pu être terrassée par l'émotion.

MAY NOT HAVE BEEN . . .ed

716. The novel may not have been translated into English.

Le roman n'a peut-être pas été traduit en anglais.

MAY HAVE BEEN . . .ing

717. You may have been playing carelessly.

Il se peut que vous ayez joué sans y faire attention.

718. They may have been bluffing.

C'était peut-être du bluff.

MAY NOT HAVE BEEN . . .ing

719.   He may not have been expecting us.

a. Il n'était peut-être pas prévenu
   de notre visite.
b. Il ne nous attendait peut-être pas.

MAY HAVE HAD to

720.   He may have had to spend the night
       there.

Peut-être a-t-il dû [qu'il a dû] y passer
la nuit.

MAY NOT HAVE HAD to

721.   They may not have had to overcome
       the same obstacles.

Ils n'ont peut-être pas dû vaincre
les mêmes obstacles.

MIGHT

Might, historically the past tense of *may*, expressing past potentiality or possibility, has popularly replaced *may* to convey these meanings in the present as well. A fairly serviceable rule of thumb is that *might* is translatable by the conditional of **pouvoir**, but this generalization oversimplifies the problem. The serious student should examine the given models with particular attention to those English sentences for which some other translation of *might* has been suggested.

722.   Better not say anything. He might
       take offense.

(Il) vaudrait mieux ne rien dire. Il
pourrait s'offenser.

723.   You might at least dust the place.

Tu pourrais au moins donner un coup
de torchon.

724.   It is less expensive than one might
       think.

C'est moins cher qu'on pourrait le
croire.

725.   Careful! The plate might be hot.

Attention! L'assiette est peut-être
chaude. [. . .peut/pourrait être chaude.]

726.   Watch how he goes about it. You
       might learn something.

Observez comment il s'y prend. Il y a
des chances pour que vous appreniez
quelque chose. [Vous pourriez
apprendre. . .]

727.   Get down off there! You might get hurt.

Descends donc! Tu risques de te faire
mal. [Tu pourrais te faire mal.]

728.   "Are you going by plane?"
       "I might."

«Tu prends l'avion? »
«C'est une possibilité.» [C'est
possible.] [Ce n'est pas exclu.]
[Je le pourrais.]

729.	He might as well know where we stand.	Autant vaudrait qu'il connaisse notre position.
730.	I had to move fast. They might come back at any minute.	Il fallait faire vite. Ils pouvaient revenir d'un moment à l'autre.
731.	I thought he might be ill.	Je croyais qu'il pouvait être malade.

In **730** and **731**, note the effect of the past situational context on the temporal value of *might* and, consequently, on the tense of **pouvoir**.

732.	There was no telling what he might do.	Il était impossible de prévoir ce qu'il ferait [pouvait faire].
733.	I was ready to sell the house at whatever price he might offer.	J'étais prêt à vendre la maison au prix qu'il offrirait, quel qu'il fût.
734.	We thought we might shoot some pool.	Nous pensions à faire un billard.
735.	He was afraid we might forget the appointment.	Il craignait que nous n'oubliions le rendez-vous.
736.	Try as he might, he couldn't loosen the nut.	Quelques efforts qu'il fît [Quoi qu'il fît] [Il avait beau s'épuiser en efforts], il ne pouvait pas desserrer l'écrou.

MIGHT NOT

737.	They might not know we are in Rouen.	Ils ne savent peut-être pas [Ils ignorent peut-être] que nous sommes à Rouen.
738.	It's true, he might not see it our way.	Il est vrai qu'il pourrait [peut] ne pas partager notre point de vue.
739.	I knew he might not consent.	Je savais qu'il pouvait [pourrait] ne pas y consentir.
740.	We were afraid we might not find you home.	Nous avions peur de ne pas vous trouver à la maison.
741.	I accepted eagerly, thinking there might not be such an opportunity soon again.	Je me suis empressé d'accepter, estimant qu'une telle occasion ne se présenterait peut-être pas de sitôt.

Depending on context, *might not* usually amounts to saying *perhaps do/does not, perhaps did not, perhaps will not,* or *perhaps would not*; hence **peut-être** plus the appropriate tense of the verb in question is always a possible translation. Note that if a form of **pouvoir** is used, the complementary infinitive, not the modal auxiliary, is negated.

MIGHT BE . . .ed

742.	I had hoped that the matter might be settled quickly.	J'avais espéré que l'affaire pourrait être vite réglée.

MIGHT NOT BE . . .ed

743. I told them they might not be
      welcomed as enthusiastically as I had
      been.

Je leur avais dit qu'ils ne seraient
peut-être pas accueillis aussi
chaleureusement que je l'avais été.

MIGHT BE . . .ing

744. There was no way of telling what might
      be going on inside.

Pas moyen de savoir ce qui pouvait se
passer à l'intérieur.

MIGHT NOT BE . . .ing

745. The trains might not be running today.

Il est possible [Il se peut que] les
trains ne circulent pas aujourd'hui.

MIGHT HAVE . . .ed

746. He might have recognized us.
      a. [= He may have recognized us / It is
         possible that he (has) recognized us.]

a. Il se peut qu'il nous ait reconnus.
   [Il nous a peut-être reconnu / Il a
   pu nous reconnaître / Il aurait pu
   nous reconnaître.]

      b. [= It was possible that he would
         recognize us.]

b. Il pouvait nous reconnaître. [Il
   était possible qu'il nous reconnaisse.]

      c. [= It was possible that he had
         recognized us.]

c. Il avait pu nous reconnaître. [Il était
   possible qu'il nous eût reconnus.]

      d. [= It is possible that, in that case,
         he would have recognized us.]

d. Il aurait pu nous reconnaître.

747. It seems to me she might have put on a
      decent outfit.

Il me semble qu'elle aurait pu s'habiller
convenablement.

748. It might have been midnight.

Il pouvait être minuit.

749. I might have known the first night
      would be sold out.

J'aurais dû savoir [me douter] qu'il
n'y aurait plus de places pour la
première.

750. I might (just) as well have stayed
      in bed.

Je serais tout aussi bien resté au lit.

751. They might have won, but for that bad
      break.

Ils avaient des chances de gagner, sans
ce coup malheureux. [Ils auraient pu
gagner. . .]

MIGHT NOT HAVE . . .ed

752.   They might not have found it.
   a. [= They may not have found it / It
       is possible that they did not find it.]

   b. [= It was possible that they would not
       find it.]

   c. [= It was possible that they had not
       found it.]

   d. [= It was possible that, in that case,
       they would not have found it.]
753.   I wonder if they might (not) already
       have found it.

   a. **Ils ne l'ont peut-être pas trouvé.**
       [**Il se peut qu'ils ne l'aient pas
       trouvé.**]

   b. **Ils pouvaient ne pas le trouver.**
       [**Ils ne le trouveraient peut-être pas.**]

   c. **Ils ne l'avaient peut-être pas trouvé.**
       [**Ils pouvaient ne pas l'avoir trouvé /
       Il était possible qu'ils ne l'eussent
       pas trouvé.**]

   d. **Ils ne l'auraient peut-être pas
       trouvé.**
**Je me demande s'ils l'auraient déjà
trouvé.**

MIGHT HAVE BEEN . . .ed

754.   If the occupants of the burning building
       had waited without opening the doors,
       they might have been saved.

**Si les occupants de l'immeuble
incendié avaient attendu sans ouvrir
les portes, ils auraient pu être sauvés.**

MIGHT NOT HAVE BEEN . . .ed

755.   His disappearance might not have been
       reported to the police.

**Sa disparition n'avait peut-être pas
été signalée à la police.**

Bear in mind that French tends to avoid bulky negative compound passives; and although examples **754** and **755** are not improbable sentences, there is danger in transferring these verb combinations to all apparently similar contexts. Consider such alternatives as replacing the passive with an active or reflexive form, or selecting a verb whose affirmative will express your idea. For example, to handle *It (a lake) might not have been destroyed*, some possibilities are: (a) **On aurait pu le sauver;** (b) **On aurait pu en empêcher la destruction;** (c) **Les poissons y nageraient peut-être encore.**

MUST   (See also HAS/HAVE to)

756.   You must pretend to enjoy it.

**Il faut que vous ayez l'air d'y
prendre plaisir.**

757.   I simply must tell you what she said.

**Il faut absolument que je te raconte
ce qu'elle a dit.**

758.	We must be tactful in dealing with them.	Il faut [faudra] les ménager.
759.	I must have them right now.	Il me les faut dès maintenant.
760.	You must think I am quite indiscreet.	Vous devez me trouver bien indiscret.
761.	It must be fun to fly one's own plane.	Cela doit être amusant de piloter son propre avion.
762.	They must have the situation well in hand.	Ils doivent avoir la situation bien en main.
763.	There must be a simpler method.	Il doit y avoir [Il y a sûrement] une méthode moins compliquée. [Il faut qu'il y ait. . .]
764.	Must you complain all the time?	Faut-il que vous vous plaigniez toujours?
765.	His proposal has some good points, you must admit.	Sa proposition n'est pas sans mérite, il faut en convenir.
766.	I must admit there is something in what he says.	Je dois avouer que ses paroles ne sont pas dépourvus de sens.
767.	I understood perfectly what I must do.	Je comprenais parfaitement ce qu'il fallait faire.
768.	I knew he must regret his decision.	Je savais qu'il devait regretter sa décision.
769.	All right, I'll leave if I must.	C'est bon, je m'en vais, puisqu'il le faut.
770.	Go ahead, read it if you must.	Allez-y, lisez-le puisque vous y tenez.

Although a distinction is usually made between the *must* of necessity (**falloir, 756-759**) and the *must* of supposition (**devoir, 760-762**), the dividing line is not rigid; at times the stronger **falloir** and the less emphatic **devoir** may be practically interchangeable (**763**).

It is important to consider the time to which invariable *must* refers, and select the French tense accordingly. The imperfect is indicated in **767** and **768**; the future may be intended in **758**.

Sentence **770** is idiomatic; *must* here has the meaning of *want to* or *feel (you) have to*.

MUST NOT

771.	You must not believe everything you are told.	Il ne faut pas croire tout ce qu'on vous dit.
772.	He must not find out where we went.	Il ne faut pas qu'il sache où nous sommes allés.
773.	He must not be hungry; he has hardly touched his food.	Il a à peine [n'a guère] touché à son repas; il ne doit pas avoir faim [il n'a évidemment pas faim].
774.	They walked away slowly; they must not attract the supervisor's attention.	Ils s'éloignèrent sans hâte; il ne fallait pas s'attirer le regard du surveillant.
775.	It must not be the same Mr. Martin.	Il s'agit sans doute d'un autre M. Martin. [Ce doit être un autre. . .]

MUST BE . . .ed

776. This mission must be carried out as soon as possible.

Il faut que cette mission soit accomplie dans le plus bref délai.

777. Dogs must be kept on the leash.

Les chiens doivent être tenus en laisse.

778. All absences must be reported to the dean.

Toute absence doit être signalée au doyen.

MUST NOT BE . . .ed

779. This part must not be given to an inexperienced actor.

Il ne faut pas que ce rôle soit confié à un comédien inexpérimenté.

780. Their influence must not be underestimated.

a. Leur influence ne doit pas être sous-estimée.

b. Il ne faut pas sous-estimer leur influence.

MUST BE . . .ing

781. They must be having a ball.

a. Ils doivent s'amuser énormément.

b. Ce qu'ils doivent s'amuser!

782. You must be coming down with a cold.

Tu dois couver un rhume.

MUST NOT BE . . .ing

783. He must not be working very hard.

Il ne doit pas travailler [Il ne travaille sans doute pas] excessivement.

MUST HAVE . . .ed

784. I must have left it at your house.

J'ai dû l'oublier [Je dois l'avoir oublié] chez vous.

785. He must have run out of money.

Il a dû épuiser son argent [Il aura épuisé. . .]

786. You must have met (one another) occasionally.

Vous avez dû [Vous deviez] vous rencontrer de temps en temps.

787. It must have been quite late.

Il devait être très tard.

788. They thought the boat must have capsized.

On croyait que le bateau avait dû chavirer.

789. One must have experienced hardship personally in order to write about it.

Il faut avoir connu soi-même la misère pour en faire le sujet d'un livre.

790.	He *must* have realized how risky it was.	Il se rendait sûrement compte à quel point c'était hasardeux.
791.	You *must* have known what the consequences would be.	Vous ne pouviez pas ignorer les conséquences de votre acte.

The modal in *must have . . .ed* is almost always the *must* of supposition; the *must* of necessity (789) is rare in this compound tense. (Compare also 279 and 280.)

Note 788. English, lacking a past form of *must*, here depends on context for temporal clarity; French, with its completely inflected **devoir**, easily makes the distinction between past and past perfect, and is careful to do so. Past situation, as usual, is shown by the imperfect (787).

Devoir, especially in the past tenses, does not accommodate stress; ways of translating emphasized *must (have . . .ed)* are suggested in 790 and 791.

MUST NOT HAVE . . .ed

792.	They must not have taken the shortcut.	Ils n'ont pas dû prendre le raccourci.
793.	He went by without stopping; he must not have seen me.	Il continua sans s'arrêter; il n'avait pas dû me voir.

See preceding note, second paragraph.

MUST (NOT) HAVE BEEN . . .ed

794.	That tree must have been struck by lightning.	Cet arbre a dû être frappé par la foudre.
795.	She must have been surprised to hear that.	Cette nouvelle a dû l'étonner.
796.	The shipment must have been delayed by the strike.	a. La grève a sans doute retardé [aura retardé] l'expédition. b. Il faut supposer que l'expédition a été retardée par la grève.
797.	He must have been transferred.	On a dû le transférer. [Il faut croire qu'on l'a transféré / . . .qu'il a été transféré.]
798.	Their subscription must not have been renewed.	a. Ils auront négligé de renouveler [décidé de ne pas renouveler] leur abonnement. b. Leur abonnement n'a évidemment pas été renouvelé.

The combination *must (not) have been . . .ed*, occasionally translatable by **devoir** plus a passive infinitive (794), is better handled by the active tense (795) or by an alternate expression of supposition.

MUST HAVE BEEN . . .ing

799.   They must have been traveling together.   Ils devaient voyager ensemble.

MUST NOT HAVE BEEN . . .ing

800.   She must not have been sticking to her diet.   Elle ne devait pas suivre son régime.

MUST HAVE HAD to

801.   He must have had to pawn his watch.   Il a dû être obligé de mettre sa montre au clou. [Il aura dû mettre. . .]

MUST NOT HAVE HAD to

802.   You must not have had to look very long.   Vous n'avez évidemment pas dû chercher longtemps.

OUGHT to   (See also SHOULD)

803.   You ought to put more time in on your studies.   Tu devrais consacrer plus de temps à tes études.

804.   He ought to be ashamed of himself.   Il devrait avoir honte.

805.   They ought to be here by now.   Ils devraient être déjà ici.

806.   One ought always to keep one's word.   On doit toujours tenir sa parole.

807.   They ought to be in Bordeaux by now. *(and perhaps they are)*   Ils doivent être à Bordeaux à présent.

808.   If you start now, you ought to be there by noon.   En partant maintenant, vous devez arriver vers midi.

809.   What shall we give her? It ought to be something nice.   Qu'est-ce qu'on lui donne? Il faudrait (que ce soit) quelque chose de chic.

Ought to, expressing obligation in a specific instance (**803, 804**) or noting the nonoccurrence of an event or the nonexistence of a situation that was reasonably to be expected (**804, 805**), is translated by the present conditional of **devoir.** The present indicative is used to convey the idea of commonly acknowledged general obligation (**806**). In **807** and **808,** *ought to* suggests neither moral requirement nor unrealized conditions, but rather the idea of probability. In reference to an as yet unaccomplished act, *ought to,* in the sense of *should, properly,* or *should, ideally,* is often rendered by the conditional of **falloir** (**809**).

OUGHT NOT to

810.	He ought not to tease her like that.	Il ne devrait pas la taquiner comme ça.
811.	It ought not to be too expensive. *(it probably isn't)*	Cela ne doit pas coûter excessivement cher.
812.	It ought not to be so expensive. *(but unfortunately it is)*	Cela ne devrait pas coûter si cher.
813.	They ought not to allow parking here.	a. Le stationnement devrait être interdit ici.
		b. On ne devrait pas permettre le stationnement.

OUGHT to BE . . .ed

814.	Exams ought to be abolished.	Les examens devraient être abolis.

OUGHT to HAVE . . .ed (See also SHOULD HAVE . . .ed))

815.	He ought to have given us a discount.	Il aurait dû (nous) le vendre au rabais.
816.	We ought to have beaten them by twenty points.	Nous aurions dû les battre par vingt points (d'écart).
817.	She ought to have been more lenient.	Elle aurait dû [devait] être plus indulgente.
818.	You ought to have said so at once.	Il fallait le dire tout de suite.
819.	They ought to have finished breakfast by now. *(they probably have)*	Ils doivent avoir fini [ont dû finir] de déjeuner à cette heure.

The standard translation of *ought to have . . .ed* is the conditional perfect of **devoir**. The imperfect is sometimes used, occasionally with a suggestion of criticism or reproof (**817**). An idiomatic equivalent, the imperfect of **falloir**, is used principally, though not exclusively, with reference to the second person. The perfect tense (of the modal or of the infinitive) in **819** is the *ought to* of probability (compare **807** and **808**).

OUGHT NOT to HAVE . . .ed

820.	He ought not to have gone out in such weather.	Il n'aurait pas dû sortir par un temps pareil.
821.	They ought not to have argued with the referee.	Ils n'auraient pas dû [ne devaient pas] discuter avec l'arbitre. [Il ne fallait pas discuter. . .]

SHALL (NOT)

822.	We shall never forget him.	Nous ne l'oublierons jamais.
823.	I shall be with you in a moment.	Je suis à vous dans un instant.
824.	"They shall not pass!"	«Ils ne passeront pas!»
825.	Shall I pour the wine?	Dois-je servir le vin? [Voulez-vous que je serve. . .?] [Faut-il que je serve. . .?]
826.	Shall we go home?	Si nous rentrions?
827.	What shall I tell him?	a. Qu'est-ce que je dois lui dire?
		b. Qu'est-ce que je lui dis?
828.	Let's take the subway, shall we?	Prenons le métro, voulez-vous?
829.	In the future, I shall expect you to conform to established practice.	Je vous demanderai désormais de respecter l'usage établi.
830.	If he does it again, I shall have to reprimand him.	S'il recommence, je serai obligé de [je devrai] le réprimander.
831.	Applicants shall submit three letters of recommendation.	Les postulants devront présenter trois lettres de recommandation.
832.	The question is, shall the U.S. recognize Red China?	La question est celle-ci: les U.S.A. doivent-ils reconnaître la Chine communiste?

In present-day conversational American English, *shall* occurs rather infrequently except in such interrogative constructions as **825-828**, where, as the translations indicate, it is not a sign of the future tense at all. Almost entirely supplanted for all persons as a future auxiliary by *will* and *am/are/is going to*, *shall* is still found in this role in careful, formal, or emphatic style (**822-824, 829, 830**). In **831**, *shall* is imperative—a legal or administrative near-equivalent of *must*; in **832** it has a value approximated in less precise language by *should*.

SHALL HAVE . . .ed

833.	Tomorrow I shall have been here a month.	Il y aura demain un mois que je suis ici.
834.	They shall not have died in vain.	Il faut qu'ils ne se soient pas sacrifiés en vain.

See note to **SHALL** examples, above. Since the common, nonfuture values of *shall* have no counterpart in a compound form, there remains little or no need for *shall have . . .ed*, and the combination is actually a rare one in informal American English.

SHOULD

Should is one of the most challenging modals to deal with, because of the great variety of ways in which it is used, and misused, in everyday language. The student is advised to read all the examples given below before selecting any one of them as a model.

835.	She should take better care of herself.	Elle devrait soigner sa santé.
836.	One should love one's fellow man.	On doit aimer son prochain.
837.	I should like to speak to him.	Je voudrais lui parler.
838.	We should be back around noon.	
	a. [= In all probability we will be back around noon.]	a. Nous devons être de retour vers midi. [En principe, nous serons de retour. . .] [Nous serons probablement de retour. . .]
	b. [= If we are conscientious, we will be back around noon.]	b. Nous devrions être de retour vers midi.

A third possibility for **838** is " = (we told him) we would be back," which of course translates: **nous serions de retour**. This use of *should* as a conditional modal has all but disappeared in American English, except in a few set expressions (**837, 849-851**: *Thank you, I should be delighted to*, etc.); and among traditionalists who observe the obsolete distinction between *would* and *should* on the basis of person.

839.	His name should be on the passenger list. *(and presumably is)*	Son nom doit figurer sur la liste des passagers.
840.	"His name should come before mine." *(but it doesn't)* "Yes, it should."	«Son nom devrait précéder le mien.» «Oui, c'est vrai.» [Oui, vous avez raison.] [Oui, en effet.]
841.	That should be easy to prove.	Cela doit [devrait] être facile à prouver.
842.	To get a good seat, one should board the train about twenty minutes before it leaves.	Pour trouver une bonne place, il faudrait [on doit] monter dans le train une vingtaine de minutes avant le départ.
843.	I know what I *should* do, but. . .	Je sais bien ce que je devrais faire. . . [Je sais bien ce qu'il faudrait faire. . .]
844.	People eat more than they should.	Les gens mangent plus qu'ils ne devraient.
845.	I didn't know if I should laugh or cry.	Je ne savais (pas) si je devais rire ou pleurer.

In all the numbered examples above, except **837**, *should* is replaceable by *ought to*. The same substitution is impossible, however, in most of the sentences which follow.

846.	If you should see him before he leaves. . .	Si vous le voyez [Au cas où vous le verriez] avant qu'il parte. . .

847. If anyone should (happen to) ask you where I am. . .

a. Si l'on venait à vous demander où je suis. . .
b. Si l'on devait vous demander. . .
c. Si par hasard on vous demandait. . .
d. Au cas où l'on vous demanderait. . .

848. "What (would we do) if they should refuse?"

"Why should they refuse?"

«Et s'ils refusaient (que ferions-nous)?» [S'ils devaient refuser?] [S'ils allaient refuser?]

«Pourquoi refuseraient-ils?» [Pourquoi veux-tu qu'ils refusent?]

849. I should think he would be *pleased.*

Il me semble que cela lui ferait plaisir.

850. I should think he *would* be pleased!

a. Je crois bien que cela lui ferait plaisir!
b. Je conçois bien que cela lui fasse plaisir!

851. I should say so! [= Yes, emphatically!]

Je pense bien!

852. There's a cab driver. He should be able to direct us to the hotel.

Voilà un chauffeur de taxi. Il saura sans doute nous indiquer l'hôtel.

853. Applications should reach us no later than March 1.

Les demandes devront nous parvenir pas plus tard que le 1er mars.

Compare **853** with **831**. *Should* in this context is a less blunt variant of *must.*

854. I would be surprised if he should come to the office on a Saturday.

Cela m'étonnerait qu'il vienne au bureau un samedi.

855. Isn't it enough that he should let you use his library?

N'est-ce pas déjà beaucoup qu'il vous permette d'utiliser sa bibliothèque?

856. That's no reason why she should take it out on me!

Ce n'est pas une raison pour qu'elle s'en prenne à moi!

857. This racket is perfectly good. Why should I buy another?

Cette raquette me sert parfaitement. Pourquoi en achèterais-je une autre?

858. I don't see why it should take them all morning.

Je ne vois pas pourquoi ils y mettraient toute la matinée.

Note particularly **857** and **858** (and compare the rejoinder of **848**). When *why should* + infinitive is a rhetorical question (or the corresponding indirect question) concerning a hypothetical act or situation which the speaker regards as unreasonable, the standard French equivalent is **pourquoi** + conditional, with no modal auxiliary. Compare the next two examples.

859. Why should the U.S. support an unpopular government?

Pourquoi les U.S.A. appuient-ils un régime discrédité? [Pourquoi faut-il que les U.S.A. maintiennent. . .?]

860. Why should we do all the dirty work?

a. Pourquoi est-ce nous qu'on charge toujours des besognes sales?

b. Comment se fait-il que les
besognes sales, c'est toujours nous
qui les faisons / devons les faire?

In **859** and **860**, in contrast to **857** and **858**, the speaker is critically questioning an existing state of affairs, hence the present indicative (or subjunctive) instead of the conditional. (English questions of this type may be introduced by *How come?*).

861. We should pick a time when everybody can come.
    Il faudrait choisir une heure qui convienne à tout le monde.

Compare **809**.

862. How should I know?
    a. Comment veux-tu que je le sache?
    b. Est-ce que je sais, moi?

863. Who should know that better than you?
    Qui serait mieux placé que vous pour le savoir?

864. You wreck the furniture and I should pay for it? No thanks!
    Vous abîmez les meubles et c'est moi qui payerais? Merci!

865. You should live so long!
    Je vous souhaite de vivre jusque-là!

866. You don't go to the concerts? You should!
    Vous n'assistez pas aux concerts? Vous avez tort!

867. What should happen but the firm goes broke!
    Ne voilà-t-il pas que la maison fait faillite!

868. I should put myself out (on his account)!
    Je vais [Je dois] me gêner (pour lui)!

869. I should tell him my business! *(said ironically)*
    Plus souvent que je lui raconterai mes affaires!

SHOULD NOT

870. They should not undertake so many things at once.
    Ils ne devraient pas entreprendre tant de choses [mener tant d'entreprises] à la fois.

871. You shouldn't talk with your mouth full.
    On ne doit pas [Il ne faut pas] parler la bouche pleine.

872. It shouldn't be hard to catch up [make up the lost time].
    Il [Ça] ne doit [devrait] pas être difficile de combler le retard.

873. Is there any reason why you shouldn't have a room of your own?
    Y a-t-il une raison pour que vous n'ayez pas une chambre privée?

874. Why shouldn't he eat fish for breakfast if he likes it?
    Pourquoi ne mangerait-il pas du poisson au petit déjeuner si ça lui plaît [si ça lui chante]?

Compare **856** and **857**.

875.	I shouldn't wonder.
876.	You shouldn't have to explain it to him again.

Cela ne m'étonnerait pas.
Il ne devrait pas être nécessaire de le lui expliquer encore. [Vous ne devriez pas être obligé de. . .]

877.	People should not have to pay for a service they don't want.

Il ne faudrait pas que les gens aient à payer un service non voulu. [Les gens ne devraient pas être forcés de payer . . . .]

SHOULD BE . . .ed

878.	White wine should be served chilled.
879.	These bushes should be cut back.

Le vin blanc doit être servi frais.
Ces arbrisseaux devraient être élagués.

In general, present or conditional of **devoir** is used depending on whether *should be . . .ed* refers to a normally or customarily expected or required action *(= is/are to be . . .ed)* (878), or to a specific instance of desirable action or change (879).

Examples of *should be . . .ed* have not been multiplied. The models under **SHOULD**, considered with the many illustrations of passive constructions throughout the book, provide the information needed for building additional sentences of this type.

SHOULD NOT BE . . .ed

880.	Scholarships should not be handed out indiscriminately.

Les bourses ne doivent [devraient] pas être décernées à tort et à travers.

See note following **879**. What determines the choice of tense here is whether the sentence is meant as a statement of principle to which all disciplined persons will naturally conform (present), or as the criticism of an actual or anticipated deviation from approved policy (conditional). See also **SHOULD NOT, MUST NOT (BE) . . .ed**, and **IS (NOT) to BE . . .ed.**

SHOULD (NOT) BE . . .ing

881.	We should be hearing from them soon.
882.	You shouldn't be wasting your time on such nonsense.

Nous devrions avoir bientôt de leurs nouvelles.
Tu ne devrais pas perdre ton temps à des bêtises pareilles.

SHOULD HAVE . . .ed

883.	He should have apologized.

Il aurait dû faire des excuses.

884. I should have begun by introducing myself.

J'aurais dû commencer par me présenter.

885. That should have cheered him up.
  a. [= That presumably cheered him up.]
  b. [= That should have cheered him up.]
    (but apparently didn't)

  a. **Cela a dû lui remonter la morale.**
  b. **Cela aurait dû lui remonter la morale.**

886. You should have thought of that sooner.

  a. **Il fallait y penser plus tôt.**
  b. **Vous auriez dû y penser plus tôt.**
  c. **Vous deviez y penser plus tôt.**

887. Someone should have taken notes.

Il aurait fallu que quelqu'un prenne des notes.

888. Why should we have lied?
  a. [= Why was it a mistake for us not to lie?]
  b. [= What makes you think there was some reason for us to lie?]
  c. [= What makes you think we lied?]

  a. **Pourquoi aurions-nous dû mentir?** [Pourquoi devions-nous mentir?]
  b. **Pourquoi aurions-nous menti?**

  c. **Pourquoi voulez-vous que nous ayons menti?**

889. How should I have known you were sleeping? [= How was I supposed to know. . .?]

Comment devais-je savoir que tu dormais?

890. Why should anyone have wanted to kill him?

Quel motif pouvait-on avoir pour le tuer?

891. I am not at all surprised that there should have been [= has been] a misunderstanding.

Je ne suis point étonné qu'il y ait eu un malentendu.

SHOULD NOT HAVE . . .ed

892. I shouldn't have bothered with it.
893. They shouldn't have thrown grenades.

Je n'aurais pas dû m'en occuper.
Ils ont eu tort de lancer des grenades. [Ils n'auraient pas dû lancer. . .]

894. You shouldn't have given up so easily.
895. One cup of tea shouldn't have kept him awake.
  a. *(but apparently it did)*

  b. *(and presumably has not)*

  c. *(and presumably had not)*

Il ne fallait pas vous décourager si vite.

  a. **Une seule tasse de thé n'aurait pas dû l'empêcher de dormir.**
  b. **Une seule tasse de thé n'a pas dû l'empêcher de dormir.**
  c. **Une seule tasse de thé n'avait pas dû [ne devait pas] l'empêcher de dormir.**

SHOULD (NOT) HAVE BEEN . . .ed

896. The fire should have been brought under
control by now.
   a. (it probably or presumably has been)

   b. (it ought to have been, but has not)
897. I should have been kept informed.
898. The doors should not have been locked.

899. She should not have been punished so
severely.

a. L'incendie a dû être maîtrisé à
l'heure actuelle.

b. L'incendie aurait dû être maitrisé. . .
On aurait dû me tenir au courant.
Les portes n'auraient pas dû [ne
devaient pas] être fermées à clef.
Il ne fallait pas [On n'aurait pas dû]
la punir si sévèrement. [On ne devait
pas / On a eu tort de la punir . . . .]

USED to

900. You used to play better than that.
901. This region used to be nothing but a
huge swamp.
902. She is wearing her hair shorter than
she used to.
903. He used to sit for hours watching TV.

Autrefois vous jouiez mieux.
Cette région n'était autrefois qu'un
vaste marais.
Elle porte les cheveux plus courts
qu'(elle ne faisait) autrefois.
Il restait assis pendant des heures
devant le téléviseur.

WILL   (See also IS/AM/ARE to)

904. You will gradually get accustomed to it.
905. Do you think she will come back some
day?
906. They will remain in lunar orbit another
twenty-four hours.
907. If it starts to rain real(ly) hard, they
will stop the game.
908. Time will tell.

Peu à peu vous vous y habituerez.
Pensez-vous qu'elle reviendra un jour?

Ils demeureront encore vingt-quatre
heures en orbite lunaire.
S'il se met à pleuvoir sérieusement,
on arrêtera le match.
Qui vivra verra.

Will is the sign of the future in **904-908**. But the word has several other roles, and automatic rendering of *will* by the French future tense will often give an incorrect translation. Examine and compare the various uses of *will* and *will not/won't* illustrated below before attempting to translate this deceptive auxiliary.

909. What will your mother say?

910. You will catch a cold in that draft.

a. Que va dire votre mère?
b. Que dira votre mère?
Tu vas t'enrhumer dans ce courant d'air.

911.	Sit down. I'll tell you all about it.	Asseyez-vous. Je vais vous conter cela.
912.	She'll be right down. At least she says she will.	Elle va descendre. Du moins, c'est ce qu'elle dit.
913.	I'll bring it right away.	Je l'apporte tout de suite.
914.	I'll drop you off at your place and meet you at the theater at 8 o'clock.	Je vous dépose chez vous et je vous retrouve au théâtre à 8 h.

Imminent future is commonly expressed in French by **aller** + infinitive (**909-912**). Immediate future is often indicated by the present (**913, 914**); compare the English *I'm sailing tomorrow, I start to work next week.*

915.	Will you help us?	Voulez-vous nous aider?
916.	Shove over a bit, will you?	Pousse-toi un peu, veux-tu?
917.	Will you be quiet!	Veux-tu bien te taire!
918.	If you will allow me. . .	a. Si vous voulez bien me permettre. . .
		b. Si vous permettez. . .
919.	If everyone will pitch in, it won't take long.	Si chacun y met du sien, ce sera vite fait.

The interrogatives of **915, 916,** and **917** are obviously not inquiries about the future, but formulas of request (in ascending order of imperativeness or impatience). In these examples, as well as in **918** and **919,** *will* has its basic sense of *willingness.*
Remember that the future cannot be used in **si** clauses unless **si** has the meaning of *whether.*

920.	At times he will be quite lucid. *(will be = is)*	Parfois il est tout à fait lucide.
921.	A camel will live for weeks without water. *(will = can)*	Le chameau peut vivre sans eau des semaines durant.
922.	The tank will hold forty liters.	Le réservoir a une capacité de quarante litres.
923.	That will do.	Cela suffit. [C'est bon.]
924.	The plane will land at Orly at 9 a.m.	L'avion doit atterrir à Orly à 9 h.
925.	I doubt that it will be very cold.	Je doute qu'il fasse très froid.
926.	I am glad your friend will be there to receive us.	Je suis content que votre ami doive être là pour nous accueillir.

Mood takes priority over tense. For want of a future subjunctive, the present tense is used to translate an English future if the subjunctive is required (**925**). When it is necessary to indicate future time unambiguously, the present subjunctive of **devoir** (sometimes **aller**) + infinitive may be used (**926**).

927.	Some people will do anything to get attention.	Il y a des gens qui feraient n'importe quoi pour se faire remarquer.
928.	I'll try it once if you will.	Moi, je veux bien m'y risquer une fois, si tu en fais autant.

WILL NOT / WON'T

The examples and explanatory notes under **WILL** are helpful in understanding the sentences hereunder.

929. If the bus is full, it won't stop here.

Si l'autobus est complet, il ne s'arrêtera pas ici.

930. We won't know until tomorrow.

Nous ne le saurons pas avant demain.

931. I hope you won't hold it against me.

J'espère que tu ne vas pas m'en vouloir.

932. He won't give me a raise.

Il ne veut pas m'augmenter.

933. Won't you come in?

Veuillez donc entrer!

934. The management will not be responsible for lost or stolen articles.

La direction n'est pas responsable des objets perdus ou volés.

935. Bears will not touch dead bodies.

Les ours ne touchent pas aux cadavres.

936. The garbage disposal won't work.

Le broyeur ne marche pas [ne veut pas marcher].

937. I won't have people talking about me like that!

Je ne supporte pas qu'on dise de telles choses sur mon compte!

WILL (NOT) BE . . .ed

938. The storeroom will be converted into a laboratory.

L'entrepôt sera [va être / doit être] transformé en laboratoire.

939. You will be called upon to help with the decorations.

Vous serez appelés à [On vous demandera d'] assister dans la décoration.

940. The price of unused tickets will not be refunded.

Les billets non utilisés ne seront pas remboursés.

WILL (NOT) BE . . .ing

941. We'll be seeing each other from time to time.

On se retrouvera [se reverra] (sans doute) de temps en temps.

942. The mailman will be coming by any minute now.

Le facteur ne tardera pas à passer [va (sûrement) venir d'un moment à l'autre].

943. I won't be working tomorrow.

Je ne compte pas travailler demain.

944. One week from now you will be taking your oral exams.

D'aujourd'hui en huit vous serez en train de passer [vous aurez commencé] les examens oraux.

Translation of the popular English pseudo-progressives must be approximate, as French has no parallel verb form.

WILL (NOT) HAVE . . .ed

945.   By tomorrow I will have forgotten everything I learned this evening.

Demain j'aurai oublié tout ce que j'ai appris ce soir.

946.   They will not have had time to rehearse.

Ils n'auront pas eu le temps de répéter.

WILL (NOT) HAVE to

947.   They will have to hold another election.

Il faudra procéder à de nouvelles élections.

948.   You will have to run to catch the boat.

Vous devrez [Il faudra] courir pour ne pas manquer le bateau.

949.   If we use paper plates, we won't have to wash dishes.

Si nous utilisons [En utilisant] des assiettes de carton, nous n'aurons pas besoin de faire la vaisselle. [. . .nous ne devrons pas faire. . ./. . .nous n'aurons pas à faire. . ./. . .nous éviterons (la nécessité) de faire. . .]

WILL HAVE to BE . . .ed

950.   His theory will have to be revised to fit the facts.

Sa théorie devra être révisée pour cadrer avec les faits.

WILL HAVE BEEN . . .ed

951.   The next time you get to France, the old five-franc coins will have been withdrawn from circulation.

Lorsque vous serez de nouveau en France, les vieilles pièces de cinq francs auront été retirées de la circulation.

WOULD

952.   If we could afford it, we would (go and) spend a couple of weeks on the Riviera.

Si nos moyens le permettaient, nous irions passer quinze jours sur la Côte d'Azur.

953.   What would you do there?

Qu'est-ce que vous y feriez?

954.   He said he would run an ad in the paper.

Il a dit qu'il passerait une annonce dans le journal.

955.   When he had nothing else to do, he would read spy stories.

Quand il n'avait rien d'autre à faire, il lisait des romans d'espionnage.

Examples **952-955** illustrate the three most common translations of *would* + infinitive: the present conditional in a result clause accompanied by a contrary-to-fact or unrealized *if* clause (or with such a hypothesis assumed); the present conditional to denote futurity with respect to the past time of a main verb; the imperfect to mark habitual or repeated past action.

956.	If you would (just) be quiet a minute. . .	**Si vous vouliez bien vous taire un instant. . .**
957.	Would you hand me that ashtray?	**Veux-tu me passer le cendrier?**
958.	What would you have me say?	**Que voulez-vous [voudriez-vous] que je dise?**

Would as used in formulas of request is not a true conditional of the verb describing the action.

959.	I was afraid he would blow up the building.	**J'avais peur [Je craignais] qu'il ne fasse [fît] sauter le bâtiment.**
960.	He wanted a job which would permit him to live near New York.	**Il voulait un poste qui lui permît d'habiter dans les environs de New York.**

The subjunctive generally takes precedence over the conditional. The subjunctive is obligatory in the noun clause following the expression of fear in **959**. It is also required after the verb **douter**: *I doubted that he would succeed* = **Je doutais qu'il réussisse.** Careful style calls for the subjunctive in **960** as well, but the conditional is sometimes encountered in this type of adjective clause; e.g., *He was trying to find a solution which would satisfy everyone* = **Il s'efforçait de trouver une solution qui plaise / plût [plairait] à tout le monde.**

961.	It was the first clash in a battle that would go on for two days and nights. *(would = was to)*	**C'était le premier heurt d'une bataille qui devait continuer pendant quarante-huit heures.**
962.	He *would* change his mind at the last minute.	**Changer d'avis au dernier moment, c'est bien de son caractère. [Qu'il change d'avis. . ., cela ne m'étonne guère.] [Il fallait qu'il change d'avis. . ., comme c'est contrariant!] [Est-ce assez embêtant qu'il change / ait changé d'avis. . .!]**

The translations suggested for **962** are not identical in meaning. The reason is that the English might be taken either as a comment on someone's undependability (the first two), or an expression of annoyance at the consequences of the criticized behavior.

963.	A large black and white bird, with a long tail? That would be a magpie.	**Un grand oiseau noir et blanc, à la queue longue? Ce sera une pie. [C'est certainement une pie.] [Ce doit être une pie.]**

964.	She would be happy to teach you to dance.	Elle vous apprendrait volontiers à danser.
965.	As luck would have it, the dockworkers were on strike that day.	Le hasard voulut qu'il y eût ce jour-là une grève des dockers.
966.	I asked him to mow the lawn and he said he would.	Je lui ai demandé de tondre le gazon, et il a dit qu'il le ferait.
967.	Would that it were true!	Si (seulement) c'était vrai!

In **967**, *would* is no longer an auxiliary verb, but an archaic equivalent of *I wish*.

WOULD NOT

968.	If I were in his place I would not submit (to their demands).	Moi, à sa place, je ne marcherais pas.
969.	The tenor declared he would not sing again at La Scala.	Le ténor déclara qu'il ne se produirait plus à La Scala.
970.	We offered to pay for the meal, but he wouldn't take a cent.	Nous voulions payer le repas, mais il n'a rien voulu accepter.
971.	There is nothing he wouldn't do to keep from getting drafted.	Il n'y a rien qu'il ne fasse [Il ferait n'importe quoi] pour éviter le service militaire.
972.	The wood was wet and wouldn't catch fire.	Le bois était mouillé et ne prenait pas feu.
973.	Wouldn't you know it would rain the day of the picnic!	Qu'il pleuve pour le pique-nique, on pouvait [on devait / il fallait] s'y attendre.

WOULD BE . . .ed

| 974. | They assured us that any defective part would be replaced free of charge. | Ils nous ont promis que toute pièce défectueuse serait remplacée gratuitement. |

WOULD BE . . .ing

| 975. | If we were in Paris we would be having an apéritif about now. | Si nous étions à Paris, nous serions en train de prendre l'apéritif à l'heure qu'il est. |

WOULD HAVE to

976. You would have to pay five dollars on account.

Il faudrait [Vous auriez à] verser un acompte de cinq dollars.

In **976, vous devriez** could also be used, but because of possible confusion with its more frequent translation of *ought to,* some unambiguous expression is generally preferred for *would have to.*

977. When you took that camp counseling job, did you know that you would have to teach swimming?

Quand vous vous êtes engagé comme assistant au camp d'été, saviez-vous que vous seriez appelé à [tenu de] donner des leçons de natation? [. . .que vous devriez. . ./. . .qu'il faudrait. . ./ . . .qu'on vous demanderait de. . .?]

WOULD NOT HAVE to

978. We wouldn't have to get up very early.

Rien ne nous obligerait à nous lever de très bonne heure. [Nous ne serions pas forcés de. . .] [Il ne serait pas nécessaire de. . .]

WOULD HAVE . . .ed

979. If I had known you needed money, I would have sent you some.

Si j'avais su que vous aviez besoin d'argent, je vous en aurais envoyé.

Note: *If I would have . . .ed* is bad English for *If I had . . .ed.*

980. But for you, he would have drowned.

Sans vous il se noyait.

The conditional perfect is the usual equivalent of *would have . . .ed* (**979**). However, the imperfect sometimes replaces it (**980**) to express vividly, as though actually occurring, an event which almost took place and would have taken place if conditions had been slightly different. This substitution of a simple past for a conditional is occasionally found in colloquial English: *One step more and I would have been done for* might be stated, . . .*I was done for* / . . .*I was a goner,* etc.

WOULD NOT HAVE . . .ed

981. There was no point in writing to them; they wouldn't have answered.

Il aurait été [était] inutile de leur écrire; ils n'auraient pas répondu.

982. If I hadn't seen the French do it, I wouldn't have thought of putting butter on sardines.

Si je ne l'avais pas vu faire par les Français [Si je n'avais pas vu les Français le faire], je n'aurais pas imaginé de beurrer les sardines.

983. I would never have suspected it.
984. Wouldn't that have been fun!

Je ne m'en serais jamais douté.
Voilà qui aurait été amusant!

WOULD HAVE to BE . . .ed

985. In that event, the summit meeting would have to be postponed.

Dans ce cas, la conférence du sommet devrait être ajournée [il faudrait ajourner la conférence].

WOULD HAVE BEEN . . .ed

986. Five minutes more, and the job would have been finished.

Encore cinq minutes, et la tâche aurait été finie [était finie].

See note to **980.**

WOULD NOT HAVE BEEN . . .ed

987. If he had kept quiet he wouldn't have been suspected.

S'il s'était tenu tranquille, il n'aurait pas été soupçonné.

WOULD HAVE HAD to

988. I didn't go because I would have had to rent a tux.

Je n'y suis pas allé parce qu'il aurait fallu [j'aurais dû / j'aurais été obligé de] louer un smoking.

WOULD NOT HAVE HAD to

989. If you had gone to lunch before noon, you wouldn't have had to wait in line.

Si tu avais déjeuné avant midi, tu n'aurais pas été obligé de faire la queue. [. . .tu n'aurais pas dû. . ./. . .il n'aurait pas été nécessaire de. . .]

SECONDARIES

For the purposes of this book, the term *secondaries* is used to designate those verbs which, followed by another verb, (1) are capable of being preceded in the same clause by a form of **HAVE** or **BE** or a *primary* [see Section 4] ; (2) may require in translation an auxiliary or semi-auxiliary, or a verb form different from that of the English.

BEGIN

990.   He begins reading right after dinner.

Il commence [se met] à lire aussitôt le dîner fini.

991.   He began by checking my blood pressure.

Il a commencé par vérifier la pression du sang.

BELIEVE

992.   The Soviets are believed (to be) planning new space flights.

Les Soviétiques prépareraient [On croit que les Soviétiques sont en train de préparer] de nouveaux exploits spatiaux.

993.   Five people are believed to have died in the explosion.

L'explosion aurait fait cinq victimes [morts].

994.   I didn't believe I could do it.

Je ne croyais pas pouvoir le faire.

995.   Her condition is not believed to be serious.

Son état n'inspire aucune crainte.

CAUSE   (See also Causatives, Section 3)

996.   What causes him to tremble like that?

Qu'est-ce qui le fait trembler comme ça?

997.   A sudden braking caused the Fiat to spin around on the wet pavement.

Un brusque coup de freins fit opérer à la Fiat un tête-à-queue sur la chaussée mouillée.

END UP

998.   He'll end up losing his job.   Il finira par perdre sa place.

EXPECT

999.   I didn't expect him to back out [. . .that he would back out] at the last minute.   Je ne m'attendais pas à ce qu'il se dérobe au dernier moment.

1000.   I (shall) expect you to dress properly. *(expect = require)*   Je prétends que vous soyez habillé convenablement.

1001.   The trip is expected to last five days.   Le voyage doit durer cinq jours.

1002.   They were expected to start this morning.   Ils devaient se mettre en route ce matin.

1003.   How do [can] you expect me to know that?   Comment voulez-vous que je sache cela?

GET / GOT to   (For has/have GOT to, see **1025** ff.)

1004.   Did you get to see the paintings?
    a. [= Was seeing the paintings part of what you did?]   a. Avez-vous vu les peintures? [Etes-vous allé voir. . .?]
    b. [= Were you able / allowed to see the paintings?]   b. Avez-vous pu voir les peintures?
    c. [= Did you get around to seeing / Did you have a chance to see the paintings?]   c. En êtes-vous arrivé à voir [Avez-vous eu l'occasion de voir] les peintures?

1005.   I hope you (will) get to spend some time in Nice.   J'espère que vous pourrez [aurez l'occasion de] passer quelques jours à Nice.

1006.   At last I'm going to get to hear that record!   Enfin je vais pouvoir écouter ce fameux disque!

1007.   He gets to ride at the company's expense.   Il voyage [a le droit de voyager] aux frais de la compagnie.

1008.   It is getting to be late.   Il commence à se faire tard.

1009.   You will get to know his habits.   Vous en viendrez à connaître ses habitudes.

1010.   I didn't get to use it.
    a. [= I had no opportunity to use it.]   a. Je n'ai pas eu l'occasion de m'en servir.
    b. [= I was not allowed to use it.]   b. On ne m'a pas permis de m'en servir.

1011.   Then I got to thinking about what you told me.   Alors je me suis mis à réfléchir à ce que vous m'aviez dit.

GET/GOT (something/someone) . . .ed   (See also Causatives, Section 3)

1012.	He is trying to get me interested in archeology.	Il veut m'intéresser à l'archéologie.
1013.	I'll be with you as soon as I get this letter written.	Je suis à vous aussitôt que j'aurai fini d'écrire cette lettre.
1014.	He got his trousers splattered.	Son pantalon a été éclaboussé.
1015.	If he opens his mouth he gets slapped.	S'il ouvre la bouche on le gifle.
1016.	They got beaten.	a. Ils ont été battus.
		b. On les a battus.
		c. Ils se sont laissé battre.
1017.	Don't get caught.	Ne vous laissez [faites] pas pincer.
1018.	She got lost.	a. Elle s'est égarée.
		b. Elle a perdu son chemin.
1019.	Now you've got me all mixed up.	a. A force de vous écouter, je ne sais plus ce que je fais.
		b. Plus je vous écoute, moins je comprends.
1020.	I didn't get the windows washed.	
	a. [= I didn't get around to washing the windows.]	a. Je n'ai pas encore lavé les fenêtres.
	b. [= I didn't have the windows washed.]	b. Je n'ai pas fait laver les fenêtres.

See **410**, and note.

GET/GOT (something/someone) . . .ing

1021.	I've got the pump working.	J'ai réussi à faire marcher la pompe.
1022.	He's got the financial committee working on it.	Il a chargé le comité des finances de s'en occuper.
1023.	We've got them guessing.	Nous avons éveillé leur curiosité.
1024.	Get going! [= Be on your way.]	Filez!

has/have GOT to   (See also HAS/HAVE to, MUST)

1025.	He has got to realize it sooner or later.	Tôt ou tard il faudra qu'il s'en rende compte.
1026.	I have simply got to find out what's going on over there.	Il faut absolument que je sache ce qui se passe là-bas.
1027.	You've got to snap out of it.	Il faut vous secouer.
1028.	First we've got to clear up some minor matters.	Nous avons quelques détails à régler d'abord.
1029.	It's got to be your mother. No one else knows you are here.	Ce ne saurait être que votre mère. Elle est seule à savoir que vous êtes ici.

am/are/is GOING to

1030. We're going to play some handball.	Nous allons faire une partie de pelote.
1031. I hope they are not going to be angry.	J'espère qu'ils ne vont pas se fâcher.
1032. You're going to get your wish.	Vous allez être servi.
1033. Are they going to start soon?	On [Ça] va commencer (bientôt)?
1034. When is he going to finish his thesis?	Quand finira-t-il [compte-t-il finir / doit-il finir] sa thèse?
1035. My daughter is going to be an actress.	Ma fille veut [a l'intention de] devenir comédienne.
1036. I am not going to work for peanuts.	Je refuse de travailler pour des prunes.

Although it is usually possible to translate *am/are/is going to* + infinitive with the present of **aller** + infinitive, the French construction normally refers to the immediate future, and relatively distant events are spoken of in the future tense. To indicate intention, determination, etc., a more precise verb is preferred (as in **1035** and **1036**).

1037. We [You, etc.] are going to have to show her around.	Il va falloir lui servir de guide.
1038. The rules are going to have to be changed.	Les règles vont devoir être modifiées.

was/were GOING to

1039. I was just going to call you.	J'allais justement vous téléphoner.
1040. He said he was going to put it on the bulletin board.	Il a dit qu'il allait l'afficher au tableau d'annonces.
1041. We didn't know what was going to happen next.	Nous ne savions pas ce qui allait arriver.
1042. I wasn't going to tell you, but since you've found out anyway...	Je n'avais pas eu l'intention de te le dire, mais puisque tu l'as su quand même...
1043. I didn't know I was going to have to testify.	Je ne savais pas que j'allais être obligé de déposer. [...que je serais appelé à déposer / qu'on allait me demander de déposer / que je devrais déposer.]
1044. They were going to let us know, one way or the other.	Ils devaient nous communiquer la réponse, quelle qu'elle fût.

In **1044**, *were going to* is a variant of *were to*, and is so treated in translation.

HAPPEN to

1045. If you happen to see Jim, tell him
       I'd like to hear from him.

Si vous venez à voir Jacques, dites-lui
que je serais content d'avoir de ses
nouvelles.

1046. Do you happen to have a corkscrew?

Est-ce que vous auriez un tire-bouchon,
par hasard?

1047. The banks happened to be closed on
       account of some local holiday.

Il se trouvait que les banques étaient
fermées pour je ne sais quelle fête
locale.

1048. If you happen to forget the words,
       make some up.

S'il vous arrive d'oublier les paroles,
inventez-en d'autres.

HEAR / HEARD

1049. I hear bells ringing.
       J'entends tinter des sonnettes.
1050. I hear them coming.
       Je les entends venir.
1051. We heard him say it.
       Nous le lui avons entendu dire.
1052. We could hear him rummaging in the
       closet.
       Nous l'entendions qui fouillait dans
       l'armoire.
1053. Have you ever heard Professor So-and-
       So tell about the time he had in Spain?
       Avez-vous jamais entendu le professeur
       Untel raconter ses aventures en Espagne?

KEEP

1054. I keep wondering where I'll be
       a year from now.
       Je me demande toujours où je me
       trouverai dans un an.
1055. He keeps staring at me.
       Il ne cesse de me fixer des yeux.
1056. They keep repeating themselves.
       Ils ne font que se répéter.
1057. Keep going straight ahead.
       Continuez droit devant vous.
1058. Prices keep going up.
       Les prix vont toujours en augmentant.

KNOW / KNOWN

1059. We knew the battle was lost.
       Nous savions la bataille perdue.
1060. She is known to have left the country.
       On sait qu'elle a quitté le pays.
1061. He is a man (who is) known to be
       dynamic.
       C'est un homme dont on sait [on
       n'ignore pas] qu'il est dynamique.
1062. He has been known to walk five miles
       to save a few cents.
       Il lui est arrivé de faire huit kilomètres
       à pied pour économiser quelques
       centimes.

LET   (See also LET/LET'S, Section 4)

1063.	Let me finish, will you?	(Mais) laissez-moi (donc) finir!
1064.	Let yourself be pampered by the French National Railway.	Laissez-vous choyer par la SNCF.[2]
1065.	Do they let you watch them make a movie?	Est-ce qu'on vous permet de regarder tourner un film?
1066.	Don't let the engine stop.	Ne laissez pas arrêter le moteur.
1067.	Don't let them kid you.	Ne t'en laisse pas conter.
1068.	They didn't let him tell his side of the story.	Ils ne lui ont pas permis de [ne l'ont pas laissé] présenter sa version de l'affaire.
1069.	I'll let you know what comes of it.	Je vous tiendrai au courant.

LIKE

1070.	What would you like to do?	Que désirez-vous faire? [Que voudriez-vous faire?]
1071.	What would you like us to do?	Que désirez-vous [voudriez-vous] que nous fassions?
1072.	He would like to run a little business of his own.	Il aimerait [voudrait] exploiter un petit fonds de commerce. [Ça lui plairait d'exploiter...]
1073.	I would like to have seen the look on his face.	J'aurais voulu voir sa tête!
1074.	He likes talking [to talk] about how tough things were when he was young.	Il parle volontiers [il aime (à) parler] des rigueurs de sa jeunesse.
1075.	He doesn't like being told what to do.	Il n'aime pas qu'on lui donne des ordres.
1076.	I would like to thank all those who have contributed.	Je tiens à remercier tous ceux qui ont contribué.
1077.	I would like nothing better than to attend your niece's recital, but I have another engagement.	Je ne demande pas mieux que d'assister au récital de votre nièce, mais ma journée est prise.

NEED

1078.	They need to be encouraged.	a. Il faudrait [faut] les encourager. b. Ils ont/auraient besoin d'être encouragés.
1079.	He need not know about it.	Pas besoin qu'il le sache.

[2]Société Nationale des Chemins de fer Français

1080.   You need not have brought them back
so soon.

Il n'était pas nécessaire de les
rapporter si vite.

REMEMBER

1081.   He doesn't remember saying that.
1082.   Remember to take along your swimming
trunks.
1083.   Did she remember to make two carbon
copies?

Il ne se souvient pas d'avoir dit cela.
N'oubliez pas d'emporter votre
caleçon de bain.
S'est-elle souvenue qu'elle devait
faire deux copies au carbone? [A-t-elle
pensé à faire. . .?]

SAID to

1084.   He is said to have spent every penny
he had.
1085.   His latest novel is said to be his
best.
1086.   He is said to be thinking of retiring.

1087.   She is said to be a hundred years old.

Il aurait dépensé jusqu'au dernier sou
de sa fortune.
Son dernier roman doit être [serait]
le meilleur qu'il ait fait.
On dit qu'il songe à prendre sa
retraite.
On lui donne cent ans.

SEE

1088.   I didn't see her get off the train.
1089.   I saw them (being) led away.
1090.   We saw entire villages wiped out in
a matter of minutes.

Je ne l'ai pas vue descendre du train.
Je les ai vu emmener.
Nous avons vu détruire en quelques
minutes des villages entiers.

If the pronoun object of *see* is also the subject of a following infinitive, as in **1088**, the
French past participle agrees with it in gender and number. This is not the case in **1089**, where
les is the object of **emmener**. In **1090**, there is no preceding direct object to be concerned
with.

SEEM

1091.   It seems to me I have read that story.

1092.   It seems there are no survivors.
1093.   The dinner seems to have turned out
quite well.

Il me semble avoir (déjà) lu ce conte.
[J'ai l'impression que j'ai déjà lu. . .]
Il n'y aurait pas de survivants.
Il paraît que le dîner a été très réussi.

STOP

1094. It has stopped raining.	**a. Il a cessé de pleuvoir.** **b. Il ne pleut plus.**
1095. Doesn't he ever stop chattering?	Ne s'arrête-t-il donc jamais de bavarder?

SUPPOSE

1096. I suppose they would be glad to get rid of it.	**Ils seraient sans doute contents d'en être débarrassés.**
1097. Do you suppose he means what he says?	**Croyez-vous qu'il parle sérieusement?**
1098. Suppose he doesn't go along with the idea. What difference would it make?	**Supposons qu'il ne marche pas. [Et s'il ne marche pas?] Qu'est-ce que cela change / changerait?**

SUPPOSED to

1099. When are they supposed to pick us up?	**Quand doivent-ils venir nous prendre?**
1100. We were supposed to read it in French.	**Nous devions le lire en français.**
1101. Red wine is not supposed to be chilled.	**Le vin rouge ne doit pas être refroidi.**
1102. You are not supposed to be here *(= You should not be here).*	**Vous ne devriez pas être ici.**
1103. We are not supposed to be collaborating.	**Nous ne sommes pas censés collaborer.**
1104. "Did you see the letter I sent to the dean?" **a.** "No, was I supposed to?" **b.** "No, am I supposed to have?"	**«Avez-vous vu la lettre que j'ai adressée au doyen? »** **a. «Non, je devais la voir? »** **b. «Non, je suis censé l'avoir vue? »** **[Non, je dois l'avoir vue?]**
1105. Weren't you supposed to get there early and open up?	**Ne deviez-vous pas arriver à l'avance pour ouvrir?**
1106. That movie is supposed to have made several million dollars. *(it reportedly has)*	**Ce film aurait rapporté plusieurs millions de dollars.**
1107. That movie was supposed to make [to have made] several million dollars. *(but it didn't)*	**Ce film devait rapporter plusieurs millions de dollars.**
1108. How am I supposed to work with all that noise?	**Comment veut-on que je travaille dans un tapage pareil?**

Since *supposed to* has a considerable variety of meanings—*expected, allowed, reported, scheduled, deemed, required,* etc.—no single translation exists for all contexts. **Devoir**, however, comes closest to providing an all-purpose equivalent.

THINK

1109.	We thought we had anticipated everything.	Nous croyions avoir tout prévu.
1110.	She thought she ought to reward me.	Elle croyait [a cru] devoir me récompenser.
1111.	I thought I could get out of it.	Je croyais [J'avais cru] pouvoir y échapper.
1112.	He is thought to be the real leader of the movement.	On estime que c'est lui [C'est lui qui serait] le véritable chef du mouvement.
1113.	I didn't think to ask him.	Je n'ai pas pensé à le lui demander.
1114.	Have you thought of taking up sailing?	Avez-vous pensé à faire de la voile?

TRY

1115.	He tries to protest.	Il veut protester.
1116.	They tried to keep me out.	Ils ont voulu m'empêcher d'entrer.
1117.	We have tried to make this program entertaining as well as instructive.	Ce programme, nous l'avons voulu amusant aussi bien qu'instructif.

Try may be translated by **vouloir** when the sense is *start to, make an attempt to* (notably in stage directions in the present tense), etc.

WANT

1118.	Do you want to look younger?	Voulez-vous [Désirez-vous] avoir l'air plus jeune?
1119.	He wants to have his say.	Il veut [Il tient à] dire son mot.
1120.	Where do you want me to put this vase?	Où veux-tu que je mette ce vase?
1121.	She doesn't want to be reminded of it.	Elle ne veut pas qu'on le lui rappelle.
1122.	I want the production rate stepped up.	Je veux que la cadence de la production soit accélérée.
1123.	They wanted me to finish the report on my own time.	Ils voulaient que je finisse le rapport en dehors de mes heures de travail.
1124.	They will undoubtedly want to take pictures.	Ils voudront sans doute prendre des photos.
1125.	I didn't want to be stuck with them.	Je ne voulais pas [ne tenais pas à] les avoir sur les bras.
1126.	Did he want to go with you?	Est-ce qu'il voulait vous accompagner?

The various possible meanings of **1126** can be expressed more precisely as follows:

a.	[= Would he have liked to go with you? *(though he didn't)*]	a. Est-ce qu'il aurait voulu vous accompagner?

b. [= Was it of his own volition that he went with you?]

c. [= Did he ask to go with you? *(nobody has gone yet)*]

d. [= Did he ask to go with you? *(you have already made the trip)*]

b. **Est-ce qu'il vous a accompagné volontairement?**

c. **A-t-il demandé à vous accompagner?**

d. **Avait-il demandé à vous accompagner?**

1127. I didn't want to mention it, but. . .

J'aurais voulu [préféré] n'en rien dire, mais. . .

1128. Did you want to see me about something?

Vous désirez me parler?

Whether *did want* in **1128** is a gentler way of saying *do you want?* or is past because the desire preceded the encounter, the question concerns the present moment and is translated accordingly.

WATCH

1129. I watched them unload the ammunition.

Je les ai regardés décharger les munitions.

1130. We watched the boxes being unloaded.

Nous avons regardé décharger les boîtes.

1131. I was watching an artist draw caricatures on the sidewalk.

Je regardais un artiste qui dessinait des caricatures sur le trottoir.

WISH

1132. He wishes he were back in England.

a. **Il voudrait être encore en Angleterre.**
b. **Il regrette de n'être plus en Angleterre.**

1133. I wish I had seen that game.

J'aurais voulu voir ce match-là. [Je voudrais avoir vu. . . .]

Note: *I wish I would have . . .ed* is incorrect English.

1134. I wish the fog would lift.

Je voudrais que le brouillard se dissipe.

1135. I wish they would invite us to dinner.

Je souhaite [Je voudrais] qu'ils nous invitent à dîner.

1136. I wish he hadn't acted so hastily.

Je voudrais qu'il n'eût pas agi si précipitamment.

1137. We wish we could do more for them.

Nous voudrions pouvoir faire davantage pour eux.

1138. I wish this week were over.

Si seulement c'était la fin de la semaine.

1139.   I don't wish to make an issue of it.   **Je ne veux pas insister.**

WONDER

1140.   I wonder what has become of him.   **Je voudrais savoir [Je me demande]**
                                                       ce qu'il est devenu.

1141.   I was wondering what to do with this   **Je me demandais (justement) ce que**
         leftover fried chicken.   **j'allais [devais] faire de ces restes de**
                                                       poulet sauté.

MISCELLANEOUS KEY WORDS

Gathered in this section are adjectives and adverbs whose translation in certain contexts may require (1) an auxiliary, modal, or semiauxiliary verb in French, where none occurs in English; or (2) a verb form different from that of the corresponding English expression.

ABLE to (See also CAN, CANNOT, COULD, COULD NOT, Section 4)

1142.	Was he able to fix your bike?	**A-t-il pu réparer ton vélo?**
1143.	Was he able to see without glasses?	**Pouvait-il voir sans lunettes?**
1144.	He wasn't able to reach the upper shelf.	**Il ne pouvait pas [Il n'a pas pu] atteindre la planche supérieure.**
1145.	Soon he was able to see them, walking silently through the woods.	**Bientôt il put les voir qui marchaient silencieusement dans le bois.**

The past indefinite of **1142** implies the occurrence of the action stemming from the capability in question; the speaker really wants to know if the repair has been effected. The past definite in the narrative context of **1145** marks the beginning moment of the capability, in contrast to the imperfect of **1143** which refers to a past state. The choice of tense in **1144** depends on whether the reference is to a lasting situation or a specific attempt.

1146.	She will be able to get up in a few days.	**Elle pourra se lever au bout de quelques jours.**
1147.	Take him up on his offer. You won't be able to get any more for it.	**Vendez au prix offert. Vous ne pourrez pas en obtenir davantage.**
1148.	If I had been able to get away sooner I would have.	**Si j'avais pu me sauver plus tôt je l'aurais fait.**
1149.	I would not have been able to answer such a question.	**Je n'aurais pas pu [su] répondre à une telle question.**
1150.	At that age, he should be able to walk by himself.	**A cet âge il devrait pouvoir marcher tout seul.**
1151.	We ought to have been able to come up with something better than that.	**Nous aurions dû pouvoir trouver mieux.**

1152.	He must not have been able to tell them apart.	Il n'a évidemment pas pu [Il n'aura pas pu] les distinguer l'un de l'autre.
1153.	He advised that we eat a good lunch before starting out, as we might not be able to find a restaurant along the way.	Il nous a conseillé de bien déjeuner avant de partir, parce que nous ne trouverions peut-être pas [nous ne pourrions peut-être pas trouver] de restaurant en route.

ABOUT to

1154.	The curtain is about to go up.	Le rideau va se lever.
1155.	I am about to give it up.	a. Je suis sur le point d'y renoncer.
		b. Je suis près d'y renoncer.
1156.	What were you about to say?	Qu'est-ce que vous alliez dire?
1157.	I am not about to cook meals for twenty people.	Je n'ai aucune intention de préparer des repas pour vingt personnes.

The negative *am/are/is not about to,* a fairly recent creation of doubtful legitimacy, has been included because of its wide use in popular speech and its increasing acceptance in respectable (if not literary) publications.

ALMOST

1158.	He almost set his beard on fire.	a. Il a failli [manqué de] mettre le feu à sa barbe.
		b. Peu s'en faut qu'il n'ait mis le feu à sa barbe.

APPARENTLY

1159.	Apparently no one debated the point.	Il semble que personne n'ait soutenu le contraire. [Personne n'aurait soutenu ....]
1160.	"He must be a millionaire." "Apparently."	«Il doit être millionaire.» «Faut croire.»
1161.	The housing situation apparently is not going to improve.	La conjoncture immobilière ne semble pas devoir s'améliorer.

BETTER

1162.	It would be better to say nothing at all.	Il vaudrait mieux ne rien dire du tout.

1163. If you get tired standing a long time,
you had better not go to the reception.

Si ça vous fatigue de rester longtemps
debout, vous feriez mieux de ne pas
assister à la réception.

CAPABLE

1164. It was feared that the samples of lunar
soil might contain microbes capable of
coming to life in the presence of the
earth's oxygen.

On craignait que les échantillons du
sol lunaire ne contiennent des microbes
pouvant se réveiller au contact de
l'oxygène terrestre.

FINALLY

1165. They finally discovered his weakness.

Ils ont fini par découvrir son point
faible.

HARDLY

1166. He had hardly begun to speak when
the riot broke out.

A peine eut-il pris la parole que la
bagarre se déclencha.

JUST

1167. She has just moved in.
1168. He had just become aware of my
presence.
1169. When we get to the airport, the plane
will have just taken off.

Elle vient de s'installer.
Il venait de s'apercevoir de ma
présence.
Au moment où nous gagnerons
l'aéroport, l'avion viendra de décoller.

Sentences **1167** and **1168** exemplify the very common idiom **venir de** in its usual tenses.
Although most grammar textbooks imply that these are the only two forms in which the idiom
exists, the future (**1169**), however infrequently needed, has its place and does occur.

1170. This is Professor Hamelot, who has
just come to us from France.

1171. When I first met him, he had just
got out of military school.

Je vous présente (monsieur) le
professeur Hamelot, qui nous arrive
de France.
Quand j'ai fait sa connaissance, il
sortait de l'école militaire.

The present and the imperfect of such verbs as **arriver, venir,** and **sortir** may in themselves
translate, respectively, *has/have just . . .ed* and *had just . . .ed.*

1172.	I was just going to [was just about to] ask you the same thing.	J'allais justement vous poser la même question.
1173.	I just happened to have my camera with me.	Justement, j'avais mon appareil (photographique).

Justement often conveys the idea of coincidence.

1174.	We were just (merely) chatting.	Nous ne faisions que causer.
1175.	He just plays [does nothing but play] golf.	Il ne fait que jouer au golf.
1176.	His car was just (barely) broken in.	Sa voiture était tout juste rodée.
1177.	He just doesn't have any gift for languages.	C'est tout simplement qu'il n'a pas de don pour les langues.
1178.	Just thinking about it scares me.	Rien que d'y penser me fait froid dans le dos.
1179.	He would just as soon be left alone.	Il aime [aimerait] autant qu'on le laisse tranquille.

LIKELY

1180.	The celebration is likely to go on all night.	La célébration peut [pourrait] très bien durer toute la nuit.
1181.	You're likely to get in(to) trouble.	Vous risquez de vous procurer des ennuis.
1182.	They are not likely to accept a check.	Il est peu probable qu'ils acceptent [qu'ils veuillent accepter] un chèque.
1183.	The money is not likely to be recovered.	Il y a peu de chances pour qu'on retrouve l'argent.
1184.	They are likely to have been slowed down by the fog.	Le brouillard les a vraisemblablement fait ralentir.
1185.	They are likely to veto any such proposal.	Ils sont susceptibles de mettre le veto à toute proposition de ce genre.

MERELY

1186.	I merely glanced at her as I went by.	Je n'ai fait que lui jeter un coup d'œil en passant.
1187.	He merely smiled, without answering.	Il s'est contenté de sourire au lieu de répondre.

NEARLY

1188.	I nearly said the wrong thing.	J'ai failli faire une gaffe.

1189.   We nearly died of thirst.

Nous avons pensé mourir de soif.

NECESSARY

1190.   Is it necessary to make so much noise?
1191.   It isn't necessary to drink in order to have a good time.

Faut-il faire tant de bruit?
Il n'est pas nécessaire [On n'a pas besoin] de boire pour s'amuser.

Do not use **falloir** to translate *is not necessary*.

NEVERTHELESS

1192.   His attitude is nevertheless disturbing.

Son attitude ne laisse pas d'être inquiétante [est quand même inquiétante].

ONLY

1193.   Only your brother would think up something like that.
1194.   You have only to flick the switch.

1195.   I am only carrying out orders.
1196.   You really should show up, if only to make Mrs. Thénard happy.

Il n'y a que ton frère pour imaginer des trucs pareils.
Vous n'avez qu'à faire jouer l'interrupteur.
Je ne fais qu'exécuter mes ordres.
Vous devriez vraiment faire acte de présence, ne serait-ce que pour faire plaisir à Madame Thénard.

PERHAPS

1197.   Perhaps they didn't receive your order.

1198.   Perhaps no one dared to contradict him.

1199.   I have perhaps not made myself clear.

Peut-être n'ont-ils pas reçu votre commande. [Ils n'ont peut-être pas reçu . . . .]
Il se peut que personne n'ait osé le contredire.
a. Je me serai mal expliqué.
b. Je me suis peut-être mal expliqué.

POSSIBLY

1200.   Possibly we will come back via Chartres.

Il est possible [Il se peut] que nous revenions (en passant) par Chartres.

1201. He couldn't possibly have swum across the river.

Il ne saurait avoir traversé le fleuve à la nage.

PROBABLY

1202. He probably didn't understand what was expected of him.

Il n'aura pas compris [Il n'a probablement pas compris] ce qu'on attendait de lui.

RATHER

1203. I would rather you paid cash.

1204. She would rather not get involved in an argument.

J'aimerais mieux [Je préfère] que vous payiez en argent liquide.
Elle aime mieux ne pas s'engager dans une discussion.

REPORTED(LY)

1205. They reportedly tried to bribe the watchman.

1206. The enemy is reported (to be) [reportedly] fleeing.

Ils auraient essayé de corrompre le gardien.
L'ennemi serait en fuite.

(NO) SOONER

1207. No sooner had she left than the gossip began.

A peine fut-elle partie qu'on se mit à potiner. [Elle ne fut pas plus tôt partie que...]

STILL

1208. They are still talking politics.

Ils sont toujours [encore] à parler politique. [Ils n'ont pas cessé de...]

SUPPOSEDLY (See also SUPPOSED to, Section 5))

1209. They are supposedly unbeatable.

1210. The Swiss climate is supposedly very healthful.

Ils passent pour être imbattables.
Le climat de la Suisse serait [doit être] très salubre.

1211.   "Is the store open evenings?"
        "Supposedly."

«Est-ce que le magasin est ouvert le soir?»
«Oui, il doit l'être.» [Oui, en principe.]

USELESS [NO USE]

1212.   I shouted and waved but it was no
        use; he couldn't see or hear me.

1213.   It's useless to try [no use trying]
        to reason with him; he is determined
        to do things his way.

J'avais beau crier et agiter le bras; il
ne me voyait ni ne m'entendait.
On a beau [Il est inutile d'] essayer de
lui faire entendre raison; il tient à
faire à sa guise.

WILLING

1214.   I am willing to take his word for it.

1215.   Are you willing to go as high as
        two hundred dollars?

1216.   No one was willing to take a chance
        on it.

1217.   "Shall we try it once?"
        "I'm willing if you are."

1218.   You can learn anything if you are
        willing to work at it.

Je veux bien le croire sur parole.
Seriez-vous prêt à aller jusqu'à
deux cents dollars?
Personne ne voulait s'y risquer.

«Si nous essayions pour voir?»
«Si tu veux, je ne dis pas non, moi.»
Vous pouvez apprendre n'importe quoi,
à condition d'y mettre de l'effort.

INDEX

The four kinds of entries are explained in the INSTRUCTIONS FOR USE, page x. The numbers refer to the first example in the division(s) illustrating the word or form in question.